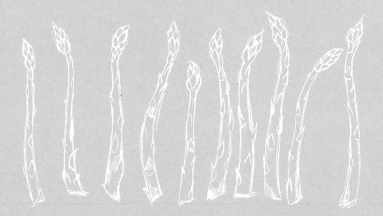

FRESH

FRESH

Simple, Delicious Recipes to Make You Feel Energized!

DONAL SKEHAN

STERLING EPICURE
New York

To Sofie, my beautiful bride, for shooting the cover photo and for not shooting me!

contents

introduction

Vegan smoothies, coconut oil, and sunrise yoga—I've lost you already, haven't I? Wait, wait. Come back. I promise this book is not solely an ode to kale and the wonders of chia seeds. Let's dial it back a little first. The world of food is ever changing. It's hard not to notice the bombardment of healthy recipes lately, including options for vegetarian, vegan, and gluten-free diets, and more. While your first reaction might be to put your nose up at all this, it is hard to avoid the facts—and with our greater knowledge of food, we need to acknowledge that the ingredients we put into our bodies really do have an effect on so many aspects of our lifestyle.

With fabulous, healthier food options and trendy new ingredients and techniques, it's essential we don't lose the connection to our knowledge of authentic home cooking and food that really tastes good. For as much as I want the benefits of a green juice pumping through my veins, I want to be excited by the food I make and to still taste those essential layers of booming flavor that excite me as a cook.

Like so many of you, my lifestyle is busy and fast-paced, often making it extremely tricky to prioritize a nutritious lunch over (*gasp!*) a fast-food burger, or a morning yoga class over a white-knuckle commute to work in rush hour traffic. Time to pull out the tiny violin: Over the last few years I've found myself frustrated and exhausted from days that start early and end late—long hours of working through the weekend, juggling/struggling through different projects, traveling, and worst of all, not having enough time to enjoy food—a First World problem, I know, but hey, it takes its toll!

Now, as someone who works in food full time, it was the most ridiculous problem—if anything, I should have been eating like a king! It felt like the most strange and disconnected problem, and it didn't sit well with me. The catalyst, and serious kick in the butt for a change in my approach to both life and food, came only recently, when I found myself barely able to stand up while filming a television show in Vietnam. Despite our guide's kind offer to visit a local miracle man and a medicinal sauna, I wound up in a Vietnamese hospital, pumped full of drugs. A week later, still feeling dreadful and now on my second round of antibiotics, I headed home to perform a string of twenty theater dates for a live-cooking tour in Ireland. I hit absolute exhaustion, a big fat concrete wall; I never knew I could be that tired and feel so awful. After this complete collapse, I vowed never to get to that place again.

These health issues became the inspiration to write a cookbook full of recipes that would tackle the exhaustion monster head on. No time to cook? Not a problem, there's a chapter on quick suppers! Suffering from a junk food snack attack? There's a whole pile of healthy snacks to tickle your taste buds. Work too busy to eat lunch? Don't be ridiculous—not when you have eighteen recipes for food on the run! I've thought of all the excuses not to make changes, and I'm sure you have, too. This cookbook is the solution.

Now we need to talk. Here's the part where I briefly divulge my inner hippie leanings. Beyond the changes I've made to eat right, I've also taken the time to reflect on just how I've been spending my time. Obviously, Vietnamese hospitals were not high on my priority list, but I learned that while stress can be a positive in our lives—pushing us to achieve—periods of stress without any recovery time was what really brought me down. I stopped saying yes to work on the weekend. I managed to stop looking at my phone every three minutes and began exercising again instead. I prioritized time spent with friends and family and, most importantly, heavens to Betsy, I made time to cook and eat the food that inspired and nourished me. Isn't that all that really matters?

Dietwise, here's the shakedown! I now aim for balanced eating, which allows me to enjoy the food I've always loved but I also put a focus on seasonal fresh fruit and vegetables, grains, and smaller amounts of high-quality meats. I take my time to cook, and I take my time to eat. (I find it helps to light a candle and put on a jazz playlist— hey, don't judge me—whatever works!) These simple but effective "rules" allow me to stay true to what I believe good home cooking ought to be.

Now, I'm not going to pretend everything's coming up roses. It takes time for any good habit to kick in—sometimes that jazz music won't play itself. It can be difficult to maintain good habits, but one of the biggest changes that worked for me is to plan ahead. Those of you out there who enjoy highlighters and Post-it notes are going to love this part: By spending time once a week shopping for ingredients, or simply writing down what you plan to make, you can really increase your chances of making better food choices. When I'm in true world-domination mode, I boil grains, wash lettuce, prepare salad dressings, bake bread, mix up marinades, toast seeds, and roast vegetables and store them for later use. I'm sure our world leaders do the same—right? These might sound like small and simple steps, but they really help me pull together a meal at the drop of a hat during the week. Shopping for ingredients plays a key part

in the process, and although I try to buy most produce as fresh as possible, I like to make sure I have plenty of other hunger-busting, meal-building ingredients waiting to burst out of my kitchen cupboards when I need them.

At its core, this book is all about simple, fresh, home-cooked food that is as nourishing as it is delicious. I've put fruits and vegetables front and center in most of the recipes and taken a worldwide journey through spice, textures, layers of flavors, and different cooking methods, all to achieve food that is both healthy and truly delicious. I'll throw my hands up and freely admit that yes, I have unashamedly used a few fashionable new ingredients and cooking methods, but only where I have tried and tested them and believe they are worth using. Don't knock a zoodle till you try one!

Even if you don't think you have time to spiralize vegetables, the chapters in this book are built for busy lifestyles. There are recipes for hearty and filling breakfasts that can be prepared in advance or cooked in a short amount of time, leaving you with a generous dose of nutrition and a side of morning sunshine! My world tends to require lunch on the go, and considering that fast food is no longer an option for me, I have written recipes for lunch options that are jam-packed with fresh and healthy ingredients and that are substantial enough to keep you going—basically the types of lunches that will make your co-workers and even the most sophisticated lunch box aficionados weep with envy. Now that you've joined me on the path of food redemption and understand that a slice of pizza in front of the television just won't cut it, there are two options for dinner: serious nourishment from a supper you can throw together with little effort in minutes or a meal that takes a little more time and allows you to savor the cooking process—this is where the jazz and candles come in. Both of these scenarios are covered here, with plenty of quick supper and relaxed dinner recipes.

Roll your eyes if you must, but the wide array of people's dietary requirements is a reality, and in this book you'll find plenty of mouthwatering recipes that offer gluten-free, dairy-free, and in some cases, sugar-free options, where, I promise, the emphasis is always on taste and flavor. Finally, in the pantry chapter, you will find staples that I believe are fundamental for lighter eating: spice mixes, healthy breads, roasted vegetables, and sauces (the "flavor makers," as I call them), all of which help to give that perfect finishing touch to your dishes. I hope you enjoy both cooking and eating them.

Now close your eyes, take a deep breath, let the mood music and warm candlelight draw you in, and let's get cooking!

the
best
meal
of the
day

While you might have disliked having breakfast cereal shoved down your throat from a young age, you have to hand it to her: your mom had it right all along! Breakfast really is the best meal of the day. While a busy world might encourage you to skip it, breakfast provides the ultimate starting point for a day of eating meals, and is full of healthy ingredients. This chapter is all about choosing the types of foods that will fill you up and keep you going throughout the day. No rumbling bellies around here! Big, dirty breakfast feasts are my jam, but, being straight up with you, I have always struggled with the drudgery of making breakfast every day—which I put down, largely, to not having a collection of recipes that excite me, either to make or to eat. There are only so many ways to make oatmeal before you want to fling it at the wall, two-year-old style. Want the good news? Breaking away from the mindless treadmill of cereal and toast doesn't have to be such a pain.

Probably the most important place to start is to mix up what you eat in morning as often as possible. Nowadays it's all about mixing it up! Between juices, smoothies, hot cereal, granola, toast toppers, healthier pancakes, and plenty of options for eggs, having a variety of breakfast options is key when it comes to breaking the cycle.

Juicing and smoothies often fall into the category of faddish diet trends, but they have both gone out of fashion and come back in again, proving they are here to stay. Both juices and smoothies provide an instant hit of nutrients, but please don't confuse one with the other. I've had more than a couple of queries about juice recipes that didn't quite work out, and when I delved a little deeper, I discovered they had been chucked into a blender. Juices should be made in a juicer, and smoothies in a blender. In this chapter, there are plenty of ideas for both, but do try to include greens as much as possible when making them. I'm head over heels in love with the Juicer Muffins on page 21, as they use up all the leftover pulp from making juices, and they're really tasty, too.

Poached Egg with Spinach, Sweet Potato Rösti and Healthy Hollandaise, or Huevos Rancheros Scrambled Eggs served on corn tortillas make for a generous weekend breakfast, while Za'atar Quinoa Poached Eggs, or Apple, Cinnamon, and Pecan Oatmeal are great, snappy everyday options. If you often find you don't have time to make a meal in the morning, these recipes are guaranteed to pull you out of bed and will convince you to carve out an extra thirty minutes at the start of the day to eat well.

Super Juices 4 Ways

Apple, Carrot, and Ginger Juice

Serves 1

2 apples

2 carrots

1 inch slice fresh ginger

Ice cubes, to serve

1. Roughly slice or chop the apples, carrots, and ginger so that they fit into your juicer's feed tube and process until you have a frothy orange liquid.

2. Pour over ice to serve. If you want more heat from the ginger, double the quantity.

Super Cleansing Juice

Serves 1

2 apples

1 carrot

1 slice lemon with rind

¼ yellow pepper, deseeded

1½ inch piece cucumber

1½ inch piece celery

1½ inch piece broccoli stem

1½ inch piece raw beet

Ice cubes, to serve

1. Roughly chop or slice the fruit and vegetables so that they fit into your juicer's feed tube.

2. Process the juice until you have a vibrant purple juice. Serve immediately over ice.

Even if you have never tried a juice before, these combinations are bound to convince you that juices with vegetables can be absolutely delicious! Sweet, zingy, and fresh with citrus or ginger, these are an incredibly healthy way to start the day.

Green Goblin Super Juice

Serves 1

2 green apples, halved if necessary

1 large handful baby leaf spinach

1 small handful kale

¾ inch slice cucumber

⅓ inch slice lime with rind

Ice cubes, to serve

1. Place one of the apples in the feed tube of your juicer and top with the spinach and kale leaves. Add the other apple to create a leafy green sandwich (this will allow you to get the maximum juice) and process.

2. Add the rest of the ingredients to the juicer and continue to juice. Pour the rich green liquid over a glass filled with ice.

Watermelon Zinger

Serves 1

½ watermelon, peeled and chopped

1½ inch piece cucumber

1 red apple

1 slice lime

1 small thumb-size piece fresh ginger

Ice cubes, to serve

1. Place all the ingredients into the feed tube of your juicer and process thoroughly.

2. Serve immediately in an ice-filled glass.

I always feel guilty dumping the pulp from my juicer into the compost bin, which is why I thought the moist pulp would be the perfect addition to a breakfast muffin. A quick search online made me realize I wasn't the first genius to think that idea up. So here goes: these are what I deem THE BEST JUICER MUFFINS in the world—tried and tested by me, my family, and my dog. We approve—let's hope you do too!

Juicer Muffins with Chocolate Glaze

1. Preheat the oven to 350°F (325°F fan) and line a 12-hole muffin pan with cupcake liners.

2. Mix all the dry ingredients together in a large mixing bowl and make a well in the center. In a large measuring cup, whisk together the syrup, milk, eggs, bananas, juicer pulp, and coconut oil. Pour the wet ingredient mixture into the dry ingredients and fold through until just combined.

3. Divide the mixture among the individual cupcake liners and bake for 25 minutes, or until they have risen and a skewer inserted in the center comes out clean. Allow the muffins to cool completely on a wire rack while you prepare the glaze.

4. In a bowl, whisk together the cocoa powder, honey, and coconut oil until you have a smooth mixture. If the coconut oil is still warm, allow the mix to cool slightly before glazing.

5. Spread each muffin with a heaping teaspoon of the glaze and sprinkle with sea salt, cacao nibs, or bee pollen. The muffins will keep for 5 days in an airtight container.

Makes 12 muffins

1 cup all-purpose flour

½ cup whole wheat flour

2⅓ cups rolled oats

3 tbsps sunflower seeds

1 tsp baking powder

1 tsp salt

5 tbsps honey or maple syrup

1 cup nut or soy milk

2 large free-range eggs

2 bananas, mashed

5 oz juicer pulp

3 tbsps coconut oil, melted

For the chocolate glaze

3 tbsps raw cocoa powder

2 tbsps honey

½ cup coconut oil, melted

Pinch of sea salt

2 tbsps raw cacao nibs or bee pollen, to decorate

Blueberry and Chia Seed Muffins

Muffins are perfect for a quick breakfast on the go. These blueberry and chia seed muffins are packed with healthy ingredients, which will keep you going on any busy morning. I normally make them the night before and grab one or two just before I leave the house.

Makes 12 muffins

1 cup all-purpose flour

½ cup whole wheat flour

2⅓ cups rolled oats

1 tsp baking powder

1 tsp ground cinnamon

3 tbsps chia seeds

1 tsp salt

½ cup brown sugar

2 bananas, mashed

2 large eggs, separated

1 cup milk

3 tbsps sunflower oil

1 cup blueberries

1. Preheat the oven to 350°F (325°F fan) and line a 12-hole muffin pan with cupcake liners.

2. In a large mixing bowl, combine both flours, rolled oats, baking powder, cinnamon, chia seeds, salt, and sugar. Create a well in the center of the dry ingredients and add the bananas, egg yolks, milk, and oil. Mix everything gently until a wet batter forms.

3. In a separate bowl, whisk the egg whites until they form soft peaks. Fold the egg whites and blueberries into the muffin batter until everything is mixed evenly.

4. Divide the muffin mixture among the cupcake liners and bake in the oven for 25 minutes, or until golden and firm to the touch.

5. The muffins will keep for 4–5 days in an airtight container. They also freeze well in resealable freezer bags.

While oatmeal always steals the show during the winter, summer is all about granola. I love the satisfaction of making up a batch of this, knowing it's ready for breakfast. I eat mine with yogurt, an extra drizzle of honey, and whatever fresh fruit I can get my hands on.

My Favorite Granola

1. Preheat the oven to 325°F (300°F fan).

2. Combine all the dry ingredients (including the dried fruit) in a large mixing bowl, drizzle the honey and coconut oil over, and mix until well combined. Tip the contents out onto a large baking tray and spread out evenly.

3. Toast in the oven for approximately 25–30 minutes, but keep an eye on it as ovens vary—you are looking for the oats to just turn a light golden brown. Give the oats a mix halfway through the cooking time to ensure an even color.

4. Remove from the oven and allow to cool on the tray before transferring to an airtight container. The granola should last up to two weeks (if you don't eat it all before then) and can be served with yogurt or milk (try soy or almond as an alternative).

Makes enough for 6–8 servings

3½ cups whole grain (old-fashioned) oats

1 cup mixed nuts (almonds, pecans, or pistachios)

1 cup pumpkin seeds

6 tbsps sunflower seeds

1 tsp ground cinnamon

½ tsp fine sea salt

About 1 cup mixed dried fruit (raisins, dried mango, dried apricots)

3 tbsps honey

3 tbsps coconut oil, melted

Breakfast Pep 'n' Power Bars

These breakfast bars are full of goodness and natural sugars—guaranteed to get you off to a good start. The mixture works well cut into bars, but can also be rolled into smaller balls.

Makes 8 bars

1½ cups ground almonds

4 tbsps almond butter

2 tbsps unsweetened cocoa powder

20 medjool dates (approx 1¼ lbs with pits or 1 lb without)

10 tbsps espresso, cooled

Pinch of sea salt

2 tbsps chia seeds

Heaping 1½ cups oats

4 tbsps dried, unsweetened coconut

To decorate

Raw cacao nibs

Toasted almonds

Dried, unsweetened coconut

Matcha green tea powder

1. Line a 5-inch square baking pan with parchment paper.

2. Place the almonds, almond butter, cocoa powder, dates, and espresso in a food processor with a pinch of sea salt and blend until you have a smooth mixture.

3. Using a spatula, fold in the chia seeds, oats, and coconut. Tip the mixture into the lined pan and press to flatten it. Cover the top with the cacao nibs, almonds, coconut, and matcha powder (use some or all of the above as you choose) and then chill in the fridge for 1 hour.

4. Remove from the pan, peel off the parchment paper, and slice into bars. Wrap in small sheets of parchment paper and tie with string.

Breakfast Toast Toppers 4 Ways

Sun-dried Tomato Pesto

Serves 4

1¼ cups sun-dried tomatoes in oil, drained

¾ cup blanched almonds

1 garlic clove, finely chopped

7 tbsps extra-virgin olive oil

3 tbsps balsamic vinegar

1 tsp cayenne pepper

Sea salt

1. Place all the ingredients in a food processor and blend until you have a smooth pesto. If the mixture is too thick, loosen with a little more olive oil.

2. Spread on toast or spoon into a serving bowl.

Guacamole

Serves 4–6

2 firm, ripe avocados

1 garlic clove, finely chopped

Juice of ½ lime, plus lime wedges to serve

1–2 dashes of Tabasco sauce

Small handful of fresh cilantro, roughly chopped, plus a few leaves to garnish

Sea salt and freshly ground black pepper

1. Slice each avocado in half, remove the pit, then spoon out the flesh into a bowl. Add the garlic, lime juice, and Tabasco, then mash with the back of a fork. (You could also do your mashing using a mortar and pestle, if you wish.)

2. When you have a rough mash, stir in the chopped cilantro. Season well with salt and pepper, then spread on toast or spoon into a serving bowl. Garnish with cilantro.

Having something smooth and creamy, yet booming with exciting color and vibrant flavors, to spread on a piece of sourdough toast or crusty bread can make a great breakfast.

Chickpea Hummus

Serves 6

2 14-oz cans chickpeas, drained and rinsed

1 garlic clove, finely chopped

1 tbsp tahini

1 tsp ground cumin

1 tsp smoked paprika

Pinch of cayenne pepper, plus extra to serve

Juice of ½ lemon

Sea salt

Extra-virgin olive oil, for drizzling

1. Tip the chickpeas into a food processor and add the garlic, tahini, cumin, paprika, cayenne pepper, lemon juice, and enough sea salt to taste. Blend until smooth; if it looks a little too stiff, simply loosen it with a little water.

2. Spread on toast or spoon into a serving bowl and serve with a drizzle of extra-virgin olive oil and a sprinkling of cayenne pepper.

Red Beet Hummus

Serves 6

4 cooked beets

1 garlic clove, roughly chopped

2 tsps ground cumin

2 tbsps pomegranate molasses, plus extra to drizzle

1 tbsp tahini

Juice of 1 lemon, plus extra if needed

Sea salt and freshly ground black pepper

2 tbsps toasted sesame seeds, to serve

1. Blend all the ingredients together, except for the sesame seeds, in a food processor until smooth. Season with salt and pepper and add a little more lemon juice to taste, if required.

2. Spread on toast or spoon into a serving bowl. Drizzle with a little more pomegranate molasses and sprinkle with the toasted sesame seeds.

Overnight Oats 4 Ways

Soaking oats overnight changes their consistency and makes them much softer. I've added chia seeds here for their jelly-like texture, which makes this breakfast more like a fancy dessert!

Raspberry and Almond

Serves 1

¼ cup rolled oats

1 tbsp chia seeds

10 tbsps almond milk

¾ cup raspberries

Coconut or plain yogurt, to serve

1 tbsp toasted sliced almonds

1. Combine the oats, chia seeds, and almond milk in a jar with a tight-fitting lid and place in the fridge overnight.

2. Blend half the raspberries with a hand-held stick blender until smooth. If you are warming the oats, heat the soaked oats gently in a small pan. Stir in the puréed raspberries and top with a generous dollop of yogurt, the remaining whole raspberries, and the toasted sliced almonds.

Strawberry and Chocolate

Serves 1

¼ cup rolled oats

1 tbsp chia seeds

10 tbsps almond milk

1 tbsp honey

1 tsp cocoa powder

4 large strawberries, hulled

Coconut or plain yogurt, to serve

1 tbsp raw cacao nibs

1. Combine the oats, chia seeds, and almond milk in a jar with a tight-fitting lid and place in the fridge overnight.

2. Mix together the honey and cocoa powder to make the chocolate sauce and set aside. Blend half the strawberries with a hand-held stick blender until smooth. If you are warming the oats, heat the soaked oats gently in a small pan. Stir in the puréed strawberries and top with a generous dollop of yogurt, the remaining strawberries, a drizzle of the chocolate sauce, and the cacao nibs.

Blueberry and Lemon

Serves 1

¼ cup rolled oats

1 tbsp chia seeds

10 tbsps almond milk

Heaping ¼ cup blueberries

Coconut or plain yogurt, to serve

Zest of ½ lemon

1. Combine the oats, chia seeds, and almond milk in a jar with a tight-fitting lid and place in the fridge overnight.

2. Blend the blueberries with a hand-held stick blender until smooth. If you are warming the oats, heat the soaked oats gently in a small pan. Swirl the puréed blueberries through the oats and top with a generous dollop of yogurt and the grated lemon zest.

Totally Tropical

Serves 1

¼ cup rolled oats

1 tbsp chia seeds

10 tbsps almond milk

1 ripe mango, peeled and thinly sliced

Coconut or plain yogurt, to serve

1 tsp dried, unsweetened coconut

Honey, for drizzling

1. ≤with a tight-fitting lid and place in the fridge overnight.

2. Blend half of the mango with a hand-held stick blender until smooth. If you are warming the oats, heat the soaked oats gently in a small pan. Stir the smooth mango through the soaked oats and top with a generous dollop of yogurt, the rest of the sliced mango, coconut, and a drizzle of honey.

Apple, Cinnamon, and Pecan Oatmeal

I am a creature of comfort and repetition: While there are many regular breakfast dishes that fall in and out of favor, I will always come back to this oatmeal with shredded apple and cinnamon. A warm hug in a bowl, this is the kind of thing you need to soothe you during the colder months of the year. I use milk in my oatmeal but you can use water instead.

Serves 1–2

Scant 1 cup rolled oats

1½ cups milk, or water if you prefer, plus extra to serve

Pinch of salt

1 apple

1 tsp ground cinnamon, plus extra to serve

2 tbsps honey, plus a drizzle to serve

Small handful of toasted pecans, roughly chopped

1. Put the oats and milk in a pan. Place over medium-high heat and bring to a boil, then reduce the heat to low. Add a pinch of salt and stir continuously until you have a thick, creamy mixture—this will take roughly 8 minutes.

2. Grate the apple (including the skin) and stir half of it into the cooked oats, then add the cinnamon and honey and mix well.

3. Pour the oatmeal into a bowl, then top it with the rest of the grated apple, some more cinnamon, and honey. Scatter the toasted pecans over the top. It's nice to add some cold milk over the top, if you like.

These semolina pancakes are great for anyone with a dairy intolerance, as they don't contain milk—if you skip the yogurt and honey to serve, they can also be vegan-friendly. Inspired by one of my favorite Dublin brunch spots, Brother Hubbard, these pancakes are light and particularly good served with slow-roasted rhubarb, yogurt, and mint.

Semolina Pancakes with Slow-roasted Rhubarb, Yogurt, and Pistachios

1. Put the semolina, yeast, baking powder, sugar, flour, and salt in a food processor. Add the lukewarm water and blend to a smooth batter. Pour the batter into a bowl, cover, and set aside in a warm place for 45 minutes, or until the batter has doubled in size and become frothy.

2. Place a large frying pan over medium-high heat. When hot, brush with a little oil. Add a scant ladleful of the batter to the pan (you should fit about 3 pancakes in the pan) and cook for 2 minutes, or until little bubbles appear on the surface. Flip and cook on the other side until golden brown. Remove from the pan and repeat the process with the remaining batter.

3. Arrange 2–3 pancakes per person on a plate and top with a dollop of yogurt and a couple of rhubarb pieces. Drizzle with honey, and sprinkle a few chopped pistachios and mint leaves over the top.

Serves 4–6

2 cups fine semolina

2½ tsps quick-rising active dry yeast

2 tsps baking powder

2 tbsps superfine sugar

1 tbsp all-purpose flour

1 tsp salt

3 cups lukewarm water

Vegetable oil, to brush

To serve

4 tbsps plain yogurt

Fragrant Roasted Rhubarb
 (see page 150)

Honey, for drizzling

Handful of chopped pistachios

Few mint leaves, torn

Gluten-free Pancakes with Blueberry, Banana, and Honey

I've been making variations on these pancakes for years, and the basic batter can be adapted with the addition of all sorts of ingredients such as nuts, seeds, chocolate, and berries. Store-bought oat flour can be used here, but I normally blend up oats in a food processor until they are a fine consistency.

Serves 2

1¼ cups oat flour (oats blended in food processor)

1 tsp gluten-free baking powder

1 tbsp chia seeds, flaxseeds, or ground pumpkin seeds

Pinch of fine sea salt

7 tbsps milk

2 large free-range eggs, separated

1 cup blueberries

1 tbsp coconut oil

1 large ripe banana, peeled and sliced

Honey, coconut yogurt, and bee pollen, to serve

1. Place all the dry ingredients in a large mixing bowl, mix to combine, and then make a well in the center. Pour the milk into a separate bowl and add the egg yolks. Whisk lightly to combine. Add to the dry ingredients and mix until blended.

2. In a clean bowl, whisk the egg whites until they hold soft peaks. Fold gently into the batter until combined. Add a handful of the blueberries to the batter, if you want, and fold them in.

3. To cook the pancakes, melt the coconut oil in a large frying pan over medium heat and add a small ladleful of the mixture to the hot pan. Cook for about 2–3 minutes on each side, or until the pancakes are golden brown. Serve the pancakes on warm plates with banana slices, blueberries, a drizzle of honey, yogurt, and bee pollen.

One of my favorite breakfasts in the whole world is Eggs Benedict—I find it pretty hard to resist if I spot it on a breakfast menu. Traditionally it's a ridiculously rich dish with a butter-laden sauce (no wonder it tastes good!), but I have been making a great alternative that swaps the heavy English muffin with a crispy, sweet potato rösti, bumps up the nutrition with some pan-fried spinach, and cuts out the butter by making a healthier hollandaise. The inspiration for the ludicrously delicious hollandaise comes from Indy Power, who writes The Little Green Spoon, a fantastic healthy-eating Irish food blog.

Poached Egg, Sweet Potato Rösti, and Healthy Hollandaise

1. Preheat the oven to 400°F (350°F fan).

2. Start with the sweet potato rösti. Place the grated sweet potato in a large bowl and crack in the egg. Season with salt and black pepper and stir well to combine. Place a large, ovenproof frying pan over medium-high heat and add the coconut oil. Place 4 heaping tablespoons of the mixture into the hot oil and press down to create little flat cakes. Fry until golden and then flip to the other side. Place the whole pan in the oven for 15–20 minutes, until cooked all the way through.

3. For the healthy hollandaise, fill a blender with boiling water while you prepare the rest of the sauce ingredients. Pour out the water when you are ready to start. The heat of the blender will help the sauce emulsify and thicken. Add the egg yolks and lemon juice, then blend until smooth. While the mixer is still on, slowly add in the melted coconut oil until the sauce is smooth and slightly thickened, then season.

4. To poach the eggs, fill a pan with about 2 inches of water, then bring to a boil. Add a pinch of sea salt and the vinegar. Lower the heat to a very gentle simmer and drop the eggs into the water right at the surface. (You may find it easier to break each egg into a cup and slide it gently into the water.) Cook for 3–4 minutes before removing with a slotted spoon and draining on paper towels.

5. Meanwhile, cook the spinach. Melt the coconut oil in a large frying pan over medium-high heat and wilt the spinach. Season with salt and pepper. Drain off any excess water and keep warm. To serve, place the sweet potato rösti on four plates, divide the spinach among them, and top each with a poached egg. Top with a generous amount of the hollandaise sauce, the chopped chives, and a grind of black pepper.

Serves 4

1 tbsp white wine vinegar

4 large free-range eggs

2 tsps coconut oil

5 cups spinach, tough stalks removed

Small handful of fresh chives, finely chopped

Sea salt and freshly ground black pepper

For the sweet potato rösti

1 large sweet potato (or 2 smaller ones), coarsely grated

1 large free-range egg

Sea salt and freshly ground black pepper

3 tbsps coconut oil

For the healthy hollandaise

2 egg yolks

Juice of ½ lemon

3 tbsps melted coconut oil

Sea salt and freshly ground black pepper

Huevos Rancheros Scrambled Eggs

This sort of breakfast, even though Mexican-inspired, always reminds me of Los Angeles, where they do really good huevos rancheros. The dish is normally comprised of fried eggs with crispy corn tortillas, refried beans, guacamole, and a tomato salsa. This is a quick and easy way of taking those fantastic Mexican flavors and transforming them into a fast and fresh breakfast.

Serves 2

4 large free-range eggs, lightly beaten

6 small corn tortillas, warmed in the oven

Sea salt and freshly ground black pepper

½ recipe Guacamole (see page 26)

For the tomato salsa

1¼ cups cherry tomatoes, diced

½ red onion, finely chopped

Small handful of fresh cilantro, roughly chopped, plus a few sprigs to garnish

Juice of ½ lime, plus wedges to garnish

Sea salt, to taste

1. Prepare the tomato salsa by combining all the ingredients together in a bowl. Season with sea salt to taste. Set aside at room temperature until needed.

2. Heat a small non-stick pan over medium-high heat and add the eggs. Lower the heat and scramble the eggs slowly until you have a thick but loose scrambled egg mixture. Remove from the heat immediately and season with sea salt and ground black pepper.

3. To serve, smear each corn tortilla with a heaping tablespoon of guacamole. Spoon in the scrambled eggs, then scatter the tomato salsa on top. Garnish with cilantro sprigs and lime wedges.

Za'atar Quinoa Poached Eggs

On a cold New York morning a few years ago, while searching for food inspiration, I got to visit a great little café called Buvette in the West Village. Sitting at the marble bar, listening to the hustle and bustle of busy New Yorkers, I had this unusual breakfast dish. Although it doesn't instantly feel like a meal for the start of the day, it makes for a dish that is as comforting as it is nutritious. The sprinkle of za'atar instantly transports the taste buds to the Middle East, while the runny poached egg, mineral-rich greens, and quinoa provide long-lasting nourishment.

Serves 2

¾ cup plus 2 tbsps quinoa

1½ cups vegetable stock

1 tbsp extra-virgin olive oil

¼ bunch kale, leaves torn from stem

3 cups spinach

1 garlic clove, finely sliced

8 cherry tomatoes, halved

3 scallions, finely sliced

½ tsp cayenne pepper

1 tsp smoked paprika

2 large free-range eggs

Sea salt

1 tbsp white wine vinegar

Za'atar (page 198), for sprinkling

1. Place the quinoa and vegetable stock in a pan and place over medium heat. Bring to a boil, then reduce the heat and simmer for about 15 minutes, or until the quinoa is cooked. Drain and set aside.

2. Heat the olive oil in a large frying pan over medium–high heat. Add the kale and fry until just softened. Add the spinach and garlic and fry until the kale and spinach have wilted. Stir in the quinoa, tomatoes, scallions, cayenne pepper, and paprika and season with sea salt. Continue to cook just until the tomatoes have softened slightly.

3. To poach the eggs, fill a pan with about 2 inches of water, then bring to a boil. Add a pinch of sea salt and the vinegar. Lower the heat to a very gentle simmer and drop the eggs into the water right at the surface. (You may find it easier to break each egg into a cup and slide it gently into the water.) Cook for 3–4 minutes before removing with a slotted spoon and draining on paper towels.

4. Serve the quinoa topped with the poached eggs and a sprinkle of za'atar.

When I was younger, most Sundays would start with the aroma of grilling bacon and sausages. By the time we made it down the stairs, my dad would be asking how we wanted our eggs—pretty good service, now that I think back! As much as the fairly irresistible smell of a traditional Irish fry can be hard to beat, even my dad has cut back on this weekly treat—more often than not, the offer is now a green smoothie! But my dad isn't the only one looking for healthy breakfast options, as proved by one of my favorite local restaurants, The House, in my hometown of Howth, which serves up this popular healthy take on the classic fry.

The House Vegetarian Fry

1. Heat about 1 teaspoon of olive oil in a frying pan over medium-high heat and fry the spinach for about 3–4 minutes, or until it has wilted down. Squeeze out any excess water and keep warm.

2. Place the frying pan back over medium-high heat with a little more olive oil. Add in the onion and garlic and fry for 5–6 minutes, or until softened. Add the canned tomatoes and oregano and season with salt and pepper. Bring to a boil, then lower the heat and simmer for 6–8 minutes. Stir in the beans and continue to cook for another 2 minutes. Transfer to a bowl and keep warm.

3. To "steam-fry" the eggs, heat about 1 teaspoon of olive oil in a large, nonstick frying pan over medium-high heat. Crack the eggs into the pan and pour in 3 tablespoons of water. Cover and cook slowly until the white is set and the yolk remains runny.

4. Place a grill pan over medium-high heat and brush with a little oil. When hot, add the tomato halves and mushrooms and cook for 3–4 minutes on each side, or until they are tender and have well-defined grill marks.

5. Serve the grilled tomatoes and mushrooms with soda bread toast, quick baked beans, spinach, and eggs. Dig in!

Serves 2

Olive oil

8⅓ cups spinach

½ red onion, finely chopped

1 garlic clove, chopped

1 14-oz can plum tomatoes

1 tsp dried oregano

1 14-oz can cannellini beans, drained and rinsed

2 large free-range eggs

2 fresh plum tomatoes, halved

4 portobello mushrooms

Sea salt and freshly ground black pepper

2 slices of whole wheat soda bread toast, to serve

Post-Workout Omelet

I like the sound of this recipe title. It makes me feel like I'm in the gym more than I possibly am! Workout or no workout, this is a seriously good omelet and one I dig into as often as I can. Mix up the filling as you wish, but I love the combination of sweet cherry tomatoes, slightly bitter colorful greens, and salty feta cheese.

Serves 1

2 tsps canola or vegetable oil

2–3 small stalks rainbow chard with leaves, roughly chopped

1 garlic clove, finely minced

3 large free-range eggs

1/3 cup feta cheese

3/4 cup cherry tomatoes, halved

2 tbsps toasted sesame seeds

Sea salt and freshly ground black pepper

1. Heat 1 teaspoon of the oil in a large, nonstick frying pan over medium-high heat and fry the chard until it is tender. When the chard is ready, stir in the garlic and continue to fry for another minute. Season to taste and transfer to a plate.

2. Whisk the eggs in a bowl until combined and season with salt and pepper.

3. Place the pan back on the heat with the remaining teaspoon of oil. Pour in the eggs and allow them to set briefly before swirling with a spatula. Add the feta cheese, rainbow chard, cherry tomatoes, and sesame seeds before folding over one half of the omelet.

4. Slide the omelet onto a plate and serve immediately.

Super Smoothies 4 Ways

Kick-ass Kale Kleaner

Serves 2

2 large handfuls of kale

2 cups freshly pressed apple juice

Juice of ½ lime

1 banana, peeled and roughly chopped

Ice cubes, to serve

1. Place all the ingredients except the ice into a blender and process until smooth (or use a pitcher and hand-held stick blender).

2. If it is too thick, add in a little extra apple juice. Pour into glasses half-filled with ice and serve.

Nutty Mango and Banana Smoothie

Serves 2

1 cup freshly squeezed orange juice

7 tbsps plain probiotic yogurt

1 ripe mango, peeled and roughly chopped

1 banana, peeled and roughly chopped

Small handful of oats

1 tbsp almond butter

Ice cubes, to serve

1. Place all the ingredients except the ice into a blender and process until smooth (or use a pitcher and hand-held stick blender).

2. Pour into glasses half-filled with ice to serve.

Smoothies are a great way to get that burst of vitamins you need in the morning, especially when using superfoods like kale (balanced here with zingy lime juice). Frozen fruit smoothies are great for kids, as the vibrant colors are super-appealing. Other fantastic smoothie ingredients include almond butter for added richness and oats to help fill you up for the day.

Frozen Red Velvet

Serves 2

1 cup freshly squeezed orange juice

1 cup frozen raspberries

1 banana, peeled and roughly chopped

1 tbsp chia seeds

3 tbsps rolled oats

1. Place all the ingredients into a blender and process until smooth (or use a pitcher and hand-held stick blender).

2. Add a little extra orange juice if you think it's a bit thick. Pour into glasses to serve.

Totally Tropical Taste Tickler

Serves 2

1 ripe mango, peeled and roughly chopped

¾ cup fresh pineapple chunks

2 tsps freshly grated ginger

2 cups coconut water

Juice of 1 lime

Ice cubes, to serve

1. Place all the ingredients except the ice into a blender and process until smooth (or use a pitcher and hand-held stick blender).

2. Pour into glasses half-filled with ice to serve.

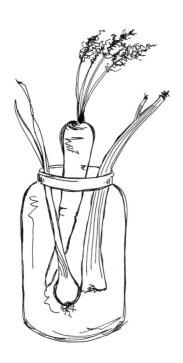

food on the go

This chapter is for all of you who start crying into your lunch boxes around 1:00 p.m., fearful that this is all life might ever amount to. I guess you could call this the SOS chapter! It's the one I rely on most heavily when it comes to eating well throughout the day and when I'm on the move, and it's the one that relies most heavily on preparation. The thing that gets to me most when I'm traveling is not having good food options. You end up being at the mercy of whatever shop, deli, or food truck you find, which is why it's essential to rise up and take back control. The majority of the recipes in this chapter fit quite happily into a lunch box or a thermos and can be eaten hot or cold, giving you lots of great choices for food on the go. Stick with me. We can get through this together!

All the salads are crunchy and crisp, ensuring no disappointing sogginess—who wants that? The salads in this book are more than a little exciting, with recipes like Cucumber Tahini Crunch Noodle Salad, with zingy dressing, toasted sesame seeds, and slippery rice noodles, or the Mini Falafel Box, with shredded salad and spiced yogurt to tantalize your taste buds. Recipes for smoky Piri Piri Chicken with Chopped Green Veggie Salad Box and crunchy Veggie Summer Rolls with Vietnamese Dipping Sauce can all be made in advance and enjoyed for lunch at work or when you're on the road.

Many of the recipes in this chapter can be made the night before, ensuring you leave the house on schedule and with every opportunity to eat well throughout the day. Take your time to enjoy preparing and choosing what you want to eat, and better food choices will become that much easier to make. Most importantly, take time to sit down and savor the food you eat—one of the most important lessons for anyone rushing through a stressful day. So no more tears . . . and best of all, you will be the envy of your co-workers!

Chunky Soups 4 Ways

Carrot and Cilantro Noodle Soup

Serves 4–6

3¾ cups chicken stock

2 garlic cloves, thinly sliced

Thumb-size piece of fresh ginger, peeled and cut into matchsticks

1 mild red chili, thinly sliced into rings

1 14-oz can light coconut milk

8 oz flat rice noodles

2 large carrots, julienned

4 tbsps chopped fresh cilantro

1 tbsp light soy sauce

Juice of 1 lime

1 tsp toasted sesame oil

1. Pour the stock into a large pan and add the garlic, ginger, and chili. Bring to a boil, stirring, and then reduce the heat and simmer for 5 minutes, until the ginger is nice and tender.

2. Add the coconut milk and rice noodles and cook until the noodles are soft, about 3 minutes.

3. Increase the heat back up to high, stir in the carrots and cook for 2 minutes, until the carrots are tender but still have a little bite. Add the cilantro (reserving a few leaves to garnish), soy sauce, lime juice, and sesame oil, and cook for another 20 seconds, then ladle into bowls. Scatter the remaining cilantro on top and serve.

Winter Root Vegetable Soup

Serves 6–8

1 tbsp butter

1 onion, chopped

1 leek, sliced

2 potatoes, peeled and chopped

2 quarts vegetable stock

2 carrots, chopped

1 parsnip, chopped

1 small celery root, peeled and chopped

Sea salt and freshly ground black pepper

Sliced brown soda bread, to serve (optional)

1. Put the butter in a large pan and place over medium-high heat. As soon as the butter has melted and is foaming, add the onion, leek, and potatoes. Sauté for 2 minutes, then cover the pan, reduce the heat, and sweat for 8 minutes.

2. Add the stock to the pan along with the carrots, parsnip, and celery root, then lower the heat and simmer for about 20 minutes, or until the vegetables are completely tender. Season to taste and then ladle into bowls. Serve with slices of brown soda bread, if you like.

I love soup's endless possibilities, and these four are a perfect testament to just that. These are a really great way to get fresh vegetables into your diet.

Spring Vegetable Minestrone

Serves 4

2 tbsps extra-virgin olive oil, plus extra to drizzle

1 bunch scallions, trimmed and finely chopped

2 garlic cloves, thinly sliced

1 fennel bulb, trimmed, halved, and finely chopped

About 2 cups mixed green vegetables (such as asparagus, zucchini, green beans, peas, and fava beans)

3 oz spaghetti, broken up into small pieces

3 cups vegetable stock (from a bouillon cube is okay)

2 tbsps basil pesto

Sea salt and freshly ground black pepper

Chopped fresh basil and flat-leaf parsley, to garnish

1. Heat the olive oil in a large pan over medium heat. Add the scallions, garlic, and fennel and gently sauté for about 10 minutes without allowing them to brown.

2. Meanwhile, prepare the green vegetables, depending on what you have—remove the woody ends from asparagus and finely slice the stalks (leave the tips whole), and trim and finely chop zucchini and green beans.

3. Add all the prepared green vegetables to the pan, then add the broken spaghetti and stock. Bring to a boil, then simmer for about 10 minutes, or until the spaghetti is just tender. Season with a little salt and pepper.

4. Ladle into big bowls and add a heaping teaspoonful of pesto. Garnish with chopped basil and parsley and drizzle with a little extra-virgin olive oil to serve.

Poached Chicken Noodle Soup

Serves 6–8

2¾ lbs whole organic chicken

2 onions, chopped

2 carrots, chopped

2 celery stalks, chopped

2 large garlic cloves, thinly sliced

Few thyme sprigs

2 fresh bay leaves

8 oz rice vermicelli noodles, broken into small pieces

Small handful each of fresh flat-leaf parsley and dill, finely chopped

Sea salt and freshly ground black pepper

1. Put the chicken into a large stockpot. Cover with cold water and place over medium-high heat. Once the water comes to a boil, reduce the heat and simmer for 30 minutes, skimming off any froth that rises to the surface.

2. Add all the vegetables to the chicken and the garlic and herbs, then season generously with salt. Bring back to a boil, then reduce the heat and simmer for 1 hour, adding the noodles for the last 10 minutes. Continue to skim the broth as necessary. Carefully remove the chicken from the pot, using tongs. Transfer to a roasting pan and leave until cool enough to handle.

3. Shred the meat off the carcass, discarding the skin and bones. Add the shredded chicken back into the soup. Add the parsley and dill, then allow to warm through. Season to taste with salt and pepper and ladle into bowls to serve.

Rainbow Beet Salad

You can get great beets these days—in fantastic colors. They are in season from June until the end of February, so keep an eye out for them at your local farmers' market. All they need is a light wash or peeling, depending on their size. Use a swivel peeler to pare them into wafer-thin slices. The horseradish in this recipe will help soften them and helps to give the salad a nice kick.

Serves 4

2 oranges

1 cup cooked red Quinoa (see page 214)

½ head Savoy cabbage, tough stalks removed and leaves roughly shredded

4 raw beets (in various colors), peeled and pared into wafer-thin slices

1 large ripe avocado, peeled, pitted, and cut into bite-size pieces

2 roasted red peppers in oil (from a jar), drained and cut into bite-size pieces

For the turmeric dressing

½ tsp ground turmeric

1 tsp freshly grated horseradish (or from a jar is fine)

2 tsps honey

Juice of ½ lemon

2 tbsps extra-virgin olive oil

Sea salt and freshly ground black pepper

1. Use a sharp knife to cut away the peel and white pith from the oranges. Cut the oranges into segments, holding them over a bowl to catch the juice, which you will use for the dressing.

2. Put the red quinoa into a large bowl and fold in the orange segments with the Savoy cabbage, beets, avocado, and roasted red peppers.

3. To make the dressing, add the turmeric, horseradish, honey, and lemon juice to the leftover orange juice (you should have about 1–2 tablespoons) and then whisk in the olive oil. Season with salt and pepper. Fold into the salad and arrange on plates to serve.

Tahini Crunch Noodle Salad

This fresh crunchy noodle salad relies on the creamy richness of a simple satay dressing to bring it to life. I often make double this recipe for a quick and light supper; the rest makes a great lunch box filler the following day.

Serves 4

2 carrots

2 large cucumbers

2 large handfuls kale (about 3½ oz), leaves torn from stem and roughly chopped

5 scallions, finely sliced

1¼ cups cooked flat rice noodles

4 tbsps sesame seeds, toasted

Small handful of fresh cilantro, roughly chopped

Small handful of fresh mint, roughly chopped

For the tahini dressing

1 chili, finely chopped

1 garlic clove, finely chopped

Thumb-size piece of fresh ginger, peeled and finely chopped

3 tbsps tahini

1 tbsp soy sauce

1 tsp sesame oil, plus extra for massaging the kale

1. Peel the carrots into long ribbons using a vegetable peeler. Do the same with the cucumbers, but turn the cucumbers and peel them from the other side when you reach the seeds in the middle (discard the seeds).

2. Whisk together the ingredients for the dressing and loosen with a few tablespoons of water until it reaches the consistency of half and half. The dressing keeps well in the fridge for up to 5 days.

3. In a large mixing bowl, massage the kale (see page 54) with a small drizzle of sesame oil until it is tender. Add the carrots, cucumber, half the scallions, noodles, half the sesame seeds, cilantro, and mint.

4. Pour over the dressing and toss until all the ingredients are evenly coated. Sprinkle the remaining sesame seeds and scallions over it to serve. This salad is great enjoyed right away, but will also keep well if made in advance.

Nutty Kale Salad with Red Cabbage, Mango, and Sesame Dressing

You may have heard of "massaging" kale and wondered what all the fuss was about. Massaging raw kale transforms it from a tough, somewhat bitter leaf into a sweet, delicate salad, and it only takes a few minutes! The combination of lime juice and salt helps to break down the cell walls in the kale, softening it and making it sweeter. So show your kale a bit of love. . . .

Serves 4

1 large bunch curly kale, tough stems removed and torn into bite-size pieces

1 tbsp lime juice

½ red cabbage, tough stalk removed, finely shredded

1 firm ripe mango, peeled, pitted, and cut into thin strips

1 mild red chili, deseeded and thinly sliced

1 tbsp chopped fresh mint

1½ tbsps chopped fresh cilantro

¼ cup toasted sliced almonds

2 tbsps toasted sesame seeds

Sea salt

For the dressing

2 tbsps light olive oil

1 tbsp toasted sesame oil

2 tbsps lime juice

1 tbsp maple syrup

1 tsp soy sauce

Sea salt and freshly ground black pepper

1. Place the kale in a large bowl with the lime juice and a good pinch of salt, and massage for 5 minutes. Add the red cabbage, mango, chili, mint, and cilantro, stirring gently to combine.

2. To make the dressing, put the olive oil, sesame oil, lime juice, maple syrup, and soy sauce in a small bowl and whisk until thickened, then season with salt and pepper. Fold the dressing into the kale salad and garnish with the almonds and sesame seeds to serve.

Puréed Soups 4 Ways

Red Lentil and Sweet Potato Soup

Serves 4–6

1 tbsp olive oil

1 small onion, finely chopped

1 carrot, finely chopped

1 celery stalk, finely chopped

Good pinch of ground allspice

1 tsp fresh thyme leaves, plus extra to garnish

1–2 red bird's-eye chilies, deseeded and finely chopped

1 large sweet potato, peeled and diced

⅓ cup split red lentils

3¾ cups chicken or vegetable stock (from a bouillion cube is okay)

Sea salt and freshly ground black pepper

4–6 tbsps crème fraîche

1. Heat the olive oil in a large pan over medium heat and sauté the onion, carrot, and celery for 5 minutes, until softened but not browned.

2. Add the allspice, thyme, and enough chili to your liking and stir for 1 minute. Add the sweet potato, lentils, and stock. Bring to a boil, then season with salt and pepper. Reduce the heat to medium, cover, and simmer for 20 minutes, until the sweet potato and lentils are completely tender.

3. Purée the soup with a hand-held stick blender, then ladle into bowls and add a dollop of crème fraîche to each one. Garnish with a little sprinkling of thyme leaves and a good grind of pepper to serve.

Carrot and Cardamom Soup with Nuts and Seeds

Serves 4–6

2 tbsps olive oil

1 large onion, thinly sliced

5 cardamom pods

Thumb-size piece of fresh ginger, peeled

1½ lbs carrots, grated (about 6 cups)

1 tbsp honey

1 tsp lemon juice

3¾ cups boiling water

Sea salt and freshly ground black pepper

Handful of mixed nuts and seeds, to garnish

1. Heat the oil in a large pan over medium heat and add the onion, stirring to coat in the oil—don't let the onions get too brown.

2. Using the flat blade of a heavy knife, lightly crush the cardamom pods and remove the seeds (discard the pods). Crush the ginger in the same way; this helps to release the juice. Add the ginger and cardamom seeds to the onion and let them sweat for 10 minutes, stirring occasionally.

3. Add the carrots, honey, and lemon juice and season generously with salt and pepper. Pour in the boiling water, bring it back to a boil, then reduce the heat and simmer for 45 minutes, until the carrots are tender.

4. Purée with a hand-held stick blender until smooth and creamy. Ladle into bowls and garnish each one with a sprinkling of the mixed nuts and seeds.

Puréed soups like these are perfect for a lunch on the go. All of them can easily be transferred to a thermos and kept warm until you're ready for them. Even though they are puréed until silky smooth, they are all full of vibrant flavors and nutrient-packed vegetables to keep you going.

Super Green Pea Soup

Serves 6

1 small ham hock
2 tbsps olive oil
1 bunch of scallions, trimmed and finely chopped
1 lb frozen peas
1 lb frozen spinach
2½ cups vegetable stock
Few mint sprigs, leaves only, roughly chopped
Sea salt and freshly ground black pepper

1. Place the ham hock in a large pan, then cover with cold water and bring to a boil. Skim off any froth that rises to the surface. Reduce the heat and simmer for about 45 minutes, or until the meat starts to pull away from the bone. Remove from the heat and let the hock cool in the liquid.

2. Once the ham hock has cooled down, remove it from the pan and set it aside. Reserve 2½ cups of the cooking liquid and discard the rest.

3. Clean the pan, add the olive oil, and place it over medium heat. Add the scallions and sauté for 2–3 minutes until softened, but not browned. Add the peas, spinach, stock, and reserved ham liquid and stir well to combine. Bring to a boil and then reduce the heat and simmer for 5 minutes.

4. Using a hand-held stick blender, blend the peas in the pan. When the soup is almost smooth, add the mint and continue to blend until smooth. Add a little more stock if the soup is too thick. Season to taste with salt and pepper. (You won't need to add much salt as the ham hock liquid will be quite salty.)

5. Remove the skin from the ham hock, cut up the meat and add it to the soup, then allow to warm through. Ladle into bowls to serve.

Tomato and Chickpea Soup

Serves 4–6

7 oz raw chorizo sausage, halved lengthwise and sliced
1 large onion, chopped
2 cups celery, chopped
2 cups carrots, chopped
2 garlic cloves, finely chopped
1 tsp smoked paprika
1 tsp mild chili powder
½ tsp ground cumin
1 14-oz can chopped tomatoes
3 cups vegetable stock (from a bouillon cube is okay)
1 14-oz can chickpeas, drained and rinsed
Sea salt and freshly ground black pepper
Extra-virgin olive oil and chopped fresh flat-leaf parsley, to garnish

1. Fry the chorizo in a large pan over medium heat until it is golden and has released its lovely spicy oil. Remove the chorizo with a slotted spoon and set it aside.

2. Add the onion, celery, and carrots to the chorizo oil in the pan, reduce the heat, and gently sauté for another 3–4 minutes. Add the garlic, paprika, chili powder, and cumin and sauté for another minute. Add the tomatoes and stock, stir well, and season with a little salt and pepper.

3. Add the chorizo and chickpeas to the pan, reserving a handful to garnish, and bring to a boil. Reduce the heat and simmer for 10–15 minutes, then purée with a hand-held stick blender until smooth. Ladle into bowls and add a drizzle of extra-virgin olive oil, the reserved chorizo and chickpeas, a good grind of black pepper, and a little chopped fresh flat-leaf parsley to serve.

This has to be the perfect transportable feast. If you're making it the night before, there is no need to refrigerate the falafel—just leave them covered at room temperature. The spiced yogurt is great to have with almost anything.

Mini Falafel Box

1. To make the falafel, place the red onion, mint, cilantro, tahini, lemon zest and juice, cumin, cayenne, and paprika in a food processor with a good pinch of salt. Pulse until finely chopped. Add the chickpeas and pulse again briefly until the chickpeas are chopped fine—you are not looking for a smooth paste but something with a bit more texture.

2. With dampened hands, shape the mixture into 20 small balls and chill in the fridge for up to an hour (if time allows). Heat a thin film of olive oil in a large nonstick frying pan over medium heat and fry the falafel balls for 4–6 minutes, until golden brown all over, turning occasionally with tongs. Drain on paper towels.

3. To prepare the shredded salad, place all the vegetables in a bowl. Make a quick dressing by whisking together the olive oil, lemon juice, honey, and a little salt and pepper (or shake in a jar with a tight-fitting lid) and then use it to dress the salad, tossing until evenly coated.

4. To make the spiced yogurt, mix all the ingredients together in a bowl. Arrange the falafel on the bulgur wheat with a small bowl of the spiced yogurt. Serve the shredded salad alongside.

Serves 4

For the falafel

½ small red onion, chopped

Small handful each of fresh mint and cilantro leaves

1 tbsp tahini

Zest and juice of ½ lemon

1 tsp ground cumin

1 tsp cayenne pepper

1 tsp smoked paprika

1 14-oz can chickpeas, drained and rinsed

Olive oil, for frying

Sea salt and freshly ground black pepper

Cooked Bulgur Wheat (see page 214), to serve

For the shredded salad

½ small head red cabbage, shredded

2 carrots, thinly sliced

½ small red onion, very thinly sliced

3 tbsps extra-virgin olive oil

Juice of ½ lemon

1 tsp honey

Sea salt and freshly ground black pepper

For the spiced yogurt

1 tsp each of ground coriander and cumin

½ tsp each of ground turmeric and mustard seeds

½ tsp chili powder

1 cup plain yogurt

1 mild red chili, thinly sliced

3 scallions, thinly sliced

Sea salt and freshly ground black pepper

Grilled Halloumi Wraps

These wraps are absolutely delicious and perfect for vegetarians. The halloumi can also be grilled. Feel free to experiment with other crunchy salad ingredients, depending on what you have on hand.

Serves 2

2 Whole Wheat Flatbreads (see page 205 or use store-bought)

2 heaping tbsps Sriracha Yogurt (see page 107)

¾ cup cooked quinoa (see page 214)

1 Little Gem lettuce, trimmed and shredded

1 ripe avocado, peeled, pitted, and chopped

Handful fresh basil leaves

For the cherry tomatoes

¾ cup cherry tomatoes, halved

1 tbsp extra-virgin olive oil

1 tsp balsamic vinegar

Sea salt and freshly ground black pepper

For the grilled halloumi

9 oz halloumi, thickly sliced

Olive oil, for brushing

Pinch of dried chili flakes

1. Start by preparing the cherry tomatoes. Preheat the oven to 375°F (350°F fan) and put the cherry tomatoes into a small roasting pan, cut side up. Drizzle with the olive oil and balsamic vinegar, and then season with salt and pepper. Roast for about 45 minutes, until the tomatoes have reduced in size and are slightly charred. Let them cool at room temperature.

2. When you are almost ready to serve, place a large, nonstick frying pan over medium-high heat. Brush the slices of halloumi with the olive oil and then sprinkle them with the dried chili flakes. Cook for 2 minutes on each side, or until golden. Transfer to a plate.

3. Wipe out the frying pan and quickly sear each whole wheat wrap for about 10 seconds on each side. Remove from the pan and then smear a tablespoon of Sriracha Yogurt down the middle of each one. Spoon on the cooked quinoa, then scatter the shredded lettuce, followed by the avocado and cooled cherry tomatoes. Tear the basil and sprinkle before finally adding the grilled halloumi. Wrap up tightly and then cut each wrap in half and serve immediately.

This is one of my favorite lunch boxes, a really tasty substantial dish that makes the most of leftover chicken. Of course, if you are looking for the ultimate quick fix, use vacuum-packed cooked beets and a can of green lentils.

Roasted Beet, Lentil, and Chicken Lunch Box

1. Preheat the oven to 400°F (350°F fan).

2. Trim away any leaves and stalks and place the beets in a roasting pan. Drizzle with vegetable oil and sprinkle the lemon zest and thyme sprigs; toss to coat. Cover the whole pan with foil and roast in the oven for about 45 minutes or so, depending on the size of the beets. When ready, the beets should be tender when pierced with a fork. Let them cool completely, then remove the skin with your fingers or a paring knife. Slice the flesh into bite-size pieces.

3. In a large bowl, whisk together the ingredients for the dressing and season with salt and pepper. Stir in the red onion and sun-dried tomatoes.

4. Place the lentils in a pan and fill it with water, then place it over high heat and bring to a boil. Reduce the heat and simmer for 20 minutes, until tender. Drain and rinse under cold water, then add the lentils to the bowl with the dressing.

5. Add the roasted beets and herbs and toss to combine. Divide among shallow bowls or transportable containers and scatter the cooked chicken on top. Stir the lemon juice into the Sriracha Yogurt and drizzle over to serve.

Serves 4

1 lb raw whole beets

1 tbsp vegetable or canola oil

Zest and juice of 1 lemon

6 fresh thyme sprigs

1 small red onion, finely diced

1 cup sun-dried tomatoes, drained and finely chopped

1¼ cups green lentils

Large handful each of cilantro, mint, and flat-leaf parsley

Shredded, cooked meat from ½ medium chicken (about 1¼ lbs)

4 tbsps Sriracha Yogurt (see page 107)

For the dressing

2 tbsps extra-virgin olive oil

1 tbsp balsamic vinegar

1 garlic clove, very finely chopped

1 tsp Dijon mustard

Sea salt and freshly ground black pepper

Curried Chicken Salad Jar

As kitsch as they may be, these curried chicken salad jars are great to have on the go. Your lunch partners may mock, but you can eat away, safe in the knowledge that deep down they're completely jealous. Mix and match the vegetables as you like, and make sure you don't overfill the jars to allow for shaking. You'll need a couple of large jars with tight-fitting lids. (Mason jars or recycled pickle jars are ideal.)

Serves 2

1 tsp olive oil

2 skinless chicken breast filets
  (about 6 oz each)

3 fresh thyme sprigs, leaves only

1 large carrot, julienned

2 celery stalks, finely diced

4 scallions, finely sliced

2 large handfuls of salad greens (arugula,
  baby spinach, baby kale, Little Gem)

Large handful of toasted almonds,
  roughly chopped

Sea salt and freshly ground black pepper

For the dressing

4 tbsps plain yogurt

1 tsp white wine vinegar

Juice of ½ lemon

2 tsps honey

1 tbsp curry powder

1 garlic clove, very finely chopped

1. Heat the oil in a large frying pan over medium-high heat. Season the chicken with salt and pepper and sprinkle with the thyme leaves. Fry for 4–6 minutes on each side, or until cooked all the way through. Remove from the pan, slice into bite-size chunks, and set aside to cool.

2. Whisk together all the ingredients for the dressing in a bowl and then add the chicken pieces, tossing to coat in the dressing.

3. Place a layer of chicken, carrot, celery, scallions, salad greens, and toasted almonds in each jar, making sure not to pack everything too tightly. When you are ready to eat, shake the jar to coat the contents. If you find eating straight from the jar a step too far, just transfer the contents to a plate when it's time to serve.

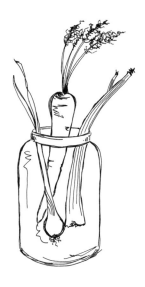

Piri Piri Chicken with Chopped Green Veggie Salad Box

If you plan on transporting this meal, or want to make it in advance, leave the avocado intact until you are ready to eat; otherwise it may discolor.

Serves 4–6

2 tbsps extra-virgin olive oil

1 tsp smoked paprika

½ tsp chopped fresh thyme

1 large garlic clove, crushed

8 boneless chicken thighs (skin on), well trimmed

Sea salt and freshly ground black pepper

For the piri piri sauce

1 large red onion, peeled and sliced in half

2 vine-ripened tomatoes, halved

3 garlic cloves

4 long fresh chilies

3 tbsps extra-virgin olive oil, plus extra for grilling

1 tbsp red wine vinegar

2 thyme sprigs

1 tsp smoked paprika

Sea salt and freshly ground black pepper

For the chopped green salad

4 scallions, finely chopped

½ cucumber, chopped

2 small ripe avocados, peeled and pitted and chopped

Large handful of sprouts, watercress, etc.

2 heads of Little Gem lettuces, chopped

1 tsp balsamic vinegar

2 tbsps extra-virgin olive oil

Sea salt and freshly ground black pepper

1. Mix 1 tablespoon of the olive oil with the paprika, thyme, garlic, and salt and pepper, then rub it all over the flesh side of the chicken thighs.

2. Place a large heavy-bottom frying pan over medium heat. Add the remaining oil to the pan, then add the chicken thighs, skin side down. Reduce the heat to very low and cook for 20–30 minutes, until the skin is nice and crispy. Don't touch them while they are cooking or shake the pan; just leave them alone, and you will produce the most fantastic crisp skin and succulent flesh. Turn the chicken thighs and let them rest in the pan with the heat off for 10 minutes before carving into slices.

3. Meanwhile, make the piri piri sauce. Place a grill pan over high heat while you toss the onion, tomatoes, garlic, and chilies in a little oil. When the pan is smoking hot, add the vegetables and char on all sides until softened and caramelized. Transfer to a food processor along with the vinegar, olive oil, thyme, and paprika and process until smooth. Season to taste with salt and pepper.

4. To make the chopped green salad, place the scallions, cucumber, avocados, watercress, and lettuce in a bowl and drizzle with vinegar and olive oil, then season with salt and pepper. Toss to coat and then divide among your plates or lunch boxes. Top with the sliced chicken thighs and serve with a bowl of the piri piri sauce.

Most large supermarkets now stock Asian foods such as rice paper wrappers. Keep them as a pantry ingredient, as they are great for a last-minute starter or snack—all you do is soak them in hot water and fill them with your favorite ingredients. This recipe is a traditional one, but you can treat rice paper wrappers as the vehicle for a whole host of healthy ingredients. Fill them with a selection of finely sliced greens, avocado, red cabbage, nuts and seeds, hot smoked salmon, or beans. The dipping sauce is an essential part of enjoying Vietnamese summer rolls, offering that subtle combination of salty, sweet, and spicy. I've added extra herbs, which isn't necessarily traditional, but adds an extra layer to this wonderful sauce.

Veggie Summer Rolls with Vietnamese Dipping Sauce

1. First make the dipping sauce. Mix the lime juice, sugar, and ½ cup water in a small bowl, stirring to dissolve the sugar. Add the fish sauce, garlic, and chilies. Taste and adjust the flavors, if necessary, to balance out the sweet and sour. Cover with plastic wrap and set aside at room temperature until needed.

2. Devein the shrimp, if necessary. If there is a black line down the back of the shrimp, use a small, sharp knife to make a shallow cut along the length of the line and carefully lift it out using the tip of the knife.

3. Place the rice paper wrappers in a heatproof bowl and cover them with hot water. Let them soak for 5 minutes, until they're soft and pliable (or prepare according to the instructions on the package).

4. Drain the wrappers on a clean dish towel and lay a few cilantro leaves along the middle of each one. Add a few leaves of mint and sweet Thai basil. Arrange 3 shrimp on each one and then scatter the cucumber, carrot, and scallions on top. Make sure you don't overfill the papers, as they may split if you do.

5. Fold in the sides of each rice paper, then roll them up to make a neat cylindrical shape. Just before serving, mix the cilantro and mint into the dipping sauce and serve immediately.

Serves 4

36 cooked Asian tiger shrimp, peeled

12 rice paper wrappers (8-inch round) or iceberg lettuce leaves

Handful of cilantro leaves

Handful of mint leaves

Handful of sweet Thai basil

1 cucumber, julienned

1 carrot, julienned

2 scallions, julienned

For the Vietnamese dipping sauce (*nuoc cham*)

3 tbsps lime juice

1 tbsp superfine sugar

2½ tbsps fish sauce (*nam pla*)

1 small garlic clove, finely minced

1–2 small Thai chilies, thinly sliced

Handful of cilantro leaves, finely chopped

Handful of mint leaves, finely chopped

Sushi Salmon and Avocado Miso Rice Bowl

This is a deconstructed sushi roll that saves you all the painstaking rolling and shaping but retains all the goodness. I've used brown sushi rice, but any short grain brown rice will work perfectly well—simply follow the instructions on the package. If you don't want to go to the bother of curing your own salmon, simply use a good-quality smoked salmon.

Serves 4

1 cup brown sushi rice

1 ripe avocado, peeled, pitted, and thinly sliced

Large handful of wild arugula leaves

1 nori sheet, sliced into thin strips

For the salmon

2 tsps Sichuan peppercorns

2 tsps coriander seeds

3 tbsps sea salt flakes or rock salt

2 tbsps sugar

1 lb organic salmon filet (from the thick end), pin bones removed, skinned, and all dark flesh removed

For the miso dressing

1 tsp spicy yellow mustard

1 tsp light miso paste

2 tsps rice vinegar

1 tsp light soy sauce

3 tbsps vegetable oil

2 tsps toasted sesame oil

1. To prepare the salmon, grind the peppercorns and coriander seeds to a coarse texture using a spice grinder or a mortar and pestle. Mix the peppercorn mixture with the salt and sugar and transfer to a large plate. Roll the salmon in the mixture until it is evenly coated. Wrap it really well with plastic wrap, place on a plate, and leave it in the fridge for 2–3 hours. The cure mixture will have drawn out some of the liquid from the fish and the flesh should feel firmer. If you are making this more than 3 hours in advance, wipe off the mixture at this point (do not rinse) then rewrap in plastic wrap and keep in the fridge until ready to use.

2. Place the rice in a pan and cover it with cold water, then let it soak for 30 minutes. Strain the rice through a sieve and then return it to the pan. Fill the pan with boiling water so that the rice is covered with about 2 inches of water. Cover the pan with a tight-fitting lid and simmer for 30–40 minutes, until all of the water has been absorbed.

3. To make the dressing, put the mustard and miso in a bowl with the vinegar and soy sauce and mix well. Slowly drizzle in the vegetable oil and the sesame oil until you have a smooth emulsion.

4. To serve, divide the brown sushi rice among 4 deep bowls. Wipe the excess cure mixture off the salmon and cut into ¼-inch-thick slices (always cut against the grain). Arrange the sliced salmon on top of the rice with slices of avocado and a small mound of arugula. Drizzle the miso dressing on top and scatter with the nori strips to serve.

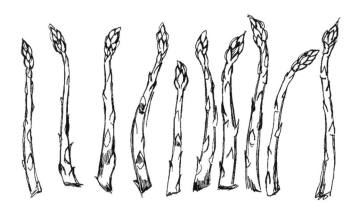

quick suppers

By the time I've finished a day at work, there's a short timeline before I get seriously "hangry." My blood sugar is low, the bets are off, and I need some proper food STAT, or I will resort to arguing about why we bought chicken instead of beef treats for the dog! Recipes for quick suppers are essential, especially when you are trying to eat lighter, fresher, and healthier meals. This is that golden moment when you have the choice between ordering in any old thing and cooking a meal that is bountiful with nutrition. The real dilemma is coming home to an empty kitchen with little to work with, so it really comes down to planning and making sure that you have the basics to rely on so that you can quickly prepare something nourishing.

Call in the quick-supper busters—recipes with big, bold flavors that never fail to excite! Here there are plenty to choose from, whether it's a vibrant salad like Tequila Chicken Quinoa Mango Salad, with a crunch from nuts and the freshness of herbs, such as coriander and mint, or the delicious, deep, dark, comfort and spice of Harissa Baked Eggs. Having recipes like these to rely on is essential to a fresh and light repertoire. Dinner options like Cilantro and Sesame Fishcakes with Spiralized Thai Salad, Tiger's Milk Sea Bass Ceviche with Quinoa Salad, and Healthy Nasi Goreng are bound to smash through the hunger barrier!

It all comes back to having a great arsenal of ingredients on hand. Keeping your kitchen cupboards well stocked with grains, beans, noodles, sauces, and spices really comes in handy when you need to make a meal quickly—and you don't have to break the bank or buy a million things every time you hit the store—all you'll need to get is some fresh vegetables or a piece of meat, chicken, or fish. This sort of thinking and planning ahead makes it a whole lot easier to make good food decisions. HUNGER BE GONE!

Basically a pimped-up fried rice, Nasi Goreng is the staple diet of backpackers and locals in Indonesia and Malaysia. Cheap to make, full of flavor, and topped with a fried egg—what's not to like? I've given it a healthy twist by unashamedly using uber-trendy cauliflower rice, which is high in vitamin C, but you could also make it with quinoa or brown rice. The backbone of the recipe begins with a vibrant paste humming with sweet and electric flavors.

Healthy Nasi Goreng

1. Devein the shrimp if necessary. If there is a black line down the back of the shrimp, use a small, sharp knife to make a shallow cut along the length of the line and carefully lift it out using the tip of the knife.

2. To make cauliflower rice, place the florets in a food processor. Process until you have a fine consistency, almost like fluffed-up couscous. Set aside.

3. Blend all the ingredients for the paste in a food processor until you have a smooth mixture. In a large wok or deep frying pan, heat 1 teaspoon of the sunflower oil over high heat. Add half of the paste and stir-fry for 1 minute, until sizzling and aromatic.

4. Add the carrot and scallions and stir-fry for 3 minutes, until just cooked through. Add the shrimp and peas and stir-fry until the shrimp are no longer translucent. Transfer to a bowl and keep warm.

5. In the same pan, heat another teaspoon of oil, if needed, and fry the remaining paste as before. Add the cauliflower rice, soy sauce, and kecap manis and fry for 3–4 minutes, or until the cauliflower rice is coated and piping hot. Return the vegetables and shrimp to the wok and toss well until hot all the way through.

6. Divide the Nasi Goreng among 4 plates and set aside while you quickly fry the eggs in the remaining oil in a clean frying pan. Serve each plateful topped with a fried egg and a sprinkling of sliced scallions and chilies.

Serves 4

10 oz raw jumbo shrimp, peeled

1 large head cauliflower, broken into florets

3 tsps sunflower oil

1 carrot, finely chopped

2 scallions, sliced, plus extra to serve

¾ cup frozen peas

1 tbsp dark soy sauce

1 tbsp kecap manis (Indonesian sweet soy sauce)

4 large eggs

1 red chili pepper, sliced, to serve

For the paste

1 tbsp peanut oil

4 garlic cloves

2 red chilies

Thumb-size piece of fresh ginger, peeled and roughly chopped

1 tbsp toasted mixed seeds

1 tsp ground turmeric

1 tsp coriander seeds

Zest and juice of 1 lime

1 tbsp fish sauce (*nam pla*)

1 tbsp ketchup

2 large shallots, peeled and roughly chopped

Harissa Baked Eggs

Whether for brunch, lunch, or dinner, these baked eggs are a speedy way to provide booming flavor and a dose of healthy comfort food. A basic tomato sauce is the hallmark of any good home cook, and here it is put to good use to coddle eggs until their yolks are runny and dreamy. With an injection of dark heat from the harissa paste, for me, this is all too often the answer to the question: "What's for dinner?"

Serves 4

1 tbsp olive oil

1 large onion, very finely diced

2 garlic cloves, very finely chopped

1 red chili, finely diced

1 tsp smoked paprika

3–4 heaping tbsps harissa paste

2 14-oz cans plum tomatoes

Large handful of cilantro, roughly chopped

4 large free-range eggs

Sea salt and freshly ground black pepper

Toasted Super Seed Bread slices (see page 202), to serve

1. Heat the olive oil in a deep ovenproof frying pan over medium heat and fry the onion for 6–8 minutes, or until softened. Add the garlic, chili, and paprika, and fry for 1–2 minutes, or until the mixture becomes aromatic.

2. Stir in the harissa paste and tomatoes, pressing the tomatoes down with the back of a fork until you are left with a smoothish consistency. Cook for 8–10 minutes at a gentle simmer, until the sauce thickens and intensifies. Season to taste. Preheat the oven to 400°F (350°F fan).

3. Stir in the cilantro, reserving a few leaves to garnish. If you want an even smoother sauce, transfer it to a food processor and blend until it is velvety, and then return the sauce to the pan (or to individual ovenproof dishes).

4. Use the back of a ladle to make 4 wells in the sauce and crack an egg into each one. Bake in the oven for 10 minutes, until the eggs are just set, but the yolks are still runny. Sprinkle the reserved cilantro on top and devour with warm toasted slices of Super Seed Bread for dipping.

Tiger's Milk Sea Bass Ceviche with Quinoa Salad

The idea of fish marinated in fruit juice might seem like an odd combination, but ceviche is having a moment, and rightly so. A fresh and vibrant traditional recipe from South America, it relies on the acidity of lime to cure the fish and infuse it with intense flavor. With only a handful of ingredients, the results are fairly impressive.

Serves 4

1⅓ lbs sea bass filets, skinned and boned

2 green chilies, finely chopped

Juice of 3 limes

Juice of 1 orange

½ red onion, finely sliced

Large handful of cilantro, roughly chopped

Sea salt

For the quinoa salad

1 cup quinoa (see page 214)

Juice of 1 lime

1 cucumber, deseeded and sliced in half moons

1¾ cups cherry tomatoes, diced

1 avocado, peeled and pitted and roughly diced

Large handful of mint leaves, roughly chopped

Large handful of cilantro, roughly chopped

Sea salt

1. Slice the fish into ¼-inch cubes, place in a bowl, and season with sea salt. Let sit for 2–3 minutes before adding the chilies and lime and orange juices. Marinate in the fridge for 10 minutes. Add the red onion and cilantro to the bowl and toss to combine.

2. Cook the quinoa and then spread out in a shallow dish to cool. When cool, squeeze in the lime juice and mix in the remaining salad ingredients. Season with sea salt to taste.

3. Serve the ceviche in individual portions with the quinoa salad on the side.

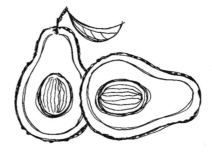

Yakitori Salmon Skewers with Red Rice Salad

The Japanese dish yakitori generally refers to skewers of chicken grilled over charcoal with a unique, smoky taste. They are often enjoyed as a street food snack with a cold beer; here I have given them a small makeover, using salmon, and serving them with a vibrant red rice salad. If you can't get your hands on red rice, use brown rice instead.

Serves 4

2 tbsps dark soy sauce

1 tbsp sake

1 tbsp mirin

1 tsp dark brown sugar

1¼ lbs skinless salmon filet, cut into 1-inch cubes

6 shiitake mushrooms, stems removed and cut into ⅓-inch slices

5 scallions, cut into 1-inch pieces

For the red rice salad

1⅓ cups red or brown rice

1 tbsp miso paste

1 tbsp mirin

1 tbsp rice vinegar

1 tsp honey

½ bunch kale leaves, torn from stem and roughly chopped

2 carrots, shaved into ribbons

½ cucumber, shaved into ribbons

2 nori sheets, sliced into strips

1 tbsp sesame seeds, toasted, to garnish

1. In a bowl, whisk together the soy sauce, sake, mirin, and brown sugar until the sugar has dissolved. Add the salmon pieces and toss to coat. Cover and chill in the fridge for about 30 minutes.

2. Thread the salmon cubes, shiitake mushrooms, and scallions onto wooden or bamboo skewers. (You should get about 2 skewers per person.) Cover and chill in the fridge for 15 minutes, or until you are ready to cook.

3. For the red rice salad, cook the rice until tender, according to the package instructions. Drain and rinse under cold water.

4. In a large bowl, whisk together the miso paste, mirin, rice vinegar, and honey. Add the kale and massage until tender. Add the carrots and cucumber ribbons, cooked rice, and nori strips.

5. When you're ready to cook the skewers, place a grill pan over high heat and cook each skewer for about 2–3 minutes on each side. Brush with any remaining marinade as they cook.

6. Sprinkle the sesame seeds over the skewers and serve with bowls of red rice salad.

Cilantro and Sesame Fishcakes with Spiralized Thai Salad

I have yet to travel to a city with more fascinating food markets than Bangkok. They can be daunting to a Western traveler at first, but there is nothing like being shuffled along by locals who know where to find the best ingredients, and discovering that every stall offers something more intriguing than the last. These vibrant fishcakes are inspired by those markets, and while a spiralized salad might not be found at many Thai street food stalls, this clever little kitchen gadget is put to good use to make a crunchy salad with a classic Thai dressing.

Serves 4

1 lb skinless white fish filets, such as haddock or cod, cut into large chunks

1 tbsp fish sauce (*nam pla*)

1 large free-range egg

1 tbsp red curry paste

1 red chili, roughly chopped

2 garlic cloves

Thumb-size piece of fresh ginger, peeled and roughly chopped

Large handful of fresh cilantro, stems and leaves, roughly chopped

Zest and juice of 1 lime

3–4 scallions, finely sliced

3 tbsps sesame seeds

2 tbsps coconut oil

Sweet chili dipping sauce, to serve

For the salad

1 tsp superfine sugar

Zest and juice of 1 lime

3 tbsps fish sauce (*nam pla*)

1 red chili, finely chopped

Large handful of peanuts, toasted

1 carrot, spiralized or julienned

1 cucumber, spiralized or julienned

3–4 scallions, finely sliced

Large handful of mint leaves, roughly chopped

1. Place the fish in a food processor and process for 3 seconds or so until smooth. Add the fish sauce, egg, curry paste, chili, garlic, ginger, cilantro, and lime zest and juice, and process again until everything is combined and the mixture begins to ball together and become thicker. Remove the blade from the food processor and stir in the scallions.

2. With damp hands, form the mixture into 12 balls and flatten to make fishcakes. Roll each one in the sesame seeds to coat.

3. Heat the coconut oil in a large frying pan over medium heat and fry the fishcakes in two batches for about 2–3 minutes on each side. Remove with a spatula and drain on a plate lined with paper towels.

4. To make the salad, whisk together the sugar, lime zest and juice, fish sauce, and chili in a large bowl until the sugar has dissolved. Crush the peanuts roughly with a mortar and pestle.

5. Add the carrot, cucumber, scallions, and mint leaves to the dressing. Toss everything together until the salad is completely coated in the dressing. Stir in the crushed peanuts, reserving about a tablespoon.

6. Serve the salad topped with the fishcakes. Drizzle with sweet chili sauce and sprinkle the reserved peanuts on top.

Pan-fried Cod with Minty Pea Purée

I love the simplicity of pan-fried fish—it's the ultimate fast food. Served with the clean flavors of peas and mint and bulked out with green lentils, this makes a snappy supper from very few ingredients.

Serves 4

4 tbsps extra-virgin olive oil

1 shallot, finely chopped

1 lb frozen peas

Small handful of mint leaves, finely chopped

1 garlic clove, finely chopped

Large handful of flat-leaf parsley leaves, finely chopped

4 cod filets (about 6 oz each), skin on

1 cup cooked green lentils

Zest and juice of 1 lemon

Sea salt and freshly ground black pepper

4 tbsps plain yogurt, to serve

1. Heat 1 teaspoon of the olive oil in a frying pan over medium-high heat, add the shallot and fry for 2–3 minutes, or until softened. Add the peas to the pan with 3 tablespoons of water and simmer for 5 minutes until the peas are just tender. Drain away any excess liquid, and then transfer the contents of the pan into the bowl of a food processor. Add the mint leaves and process until completely smooth. Season to taste.

2. In a small bowl, whisk together 3 tablespoons of the olive oil with the garlic and parsley. Season the cod filets with salt and pepper.

3. Heat the remaining olive oil in a large frying pan over medium-high heat and fry the cod, skin side down, for 4–5 minutes, depending on the thickness of the filets. Carefully turn over and continue to cook for 1–2 minutes, or until just cooked through (the flesh should be just opaque).

4. Warm the lentils in a pan and mix in the lemon zest and juice and all but 1 tablespoon of the parsley oil.

5. Spread the pea purée on serving plates, top with the lentils, and place a cod filet on top. Add a dollop of yogurt to each cod filet and drizzle with the remaining parsley oil. Serve immediately.

Pea, Asparagus, and Ricotta Frittata

Simple greens wrapped up with creamy ricotta and just-set eggs are one of the quickest suppers to make. This is a dish that is also impressive-looking enough to serve as a dinner party starter.

Serves 4

Small bunch of asparagus, ends trimmed

6 scallions, trimmed

8 large free-range eggs

¼ cup goat milk

Small handful of basil, roughly chopped, plus a few leaves to garnish

Zest of 1 lemon

½ cup frozen peas, defrosted

1 tsp olive oil

Scant ½ cup ricotta cheese

Sea salt and freshly ground black pepper

1. Blanch the asparagus and scallions for 1–2 minutes in a pan of boiling salted water. Drain and refresh in a bowl of ice-cold water.

2. In a bowl, whisk the eggs and milk together, and then season and stir in the basil, lemon zest, and peas.

3. Turn on the broiler.

4. Heat the olive oil in a large nonstick frying pan and pour in the egg mixture. Working quickly, arrange the asparagus and scallions over the top of the frittata, and dot with teaspoons of ricotta. Cook gently until the mixture is set, but still a little runny in the center. Place the pan under the broiler and cook until the egg on top is golden and bubbling.

5. Serve in big chunky quarters with a smattering of basil leaves. Season to taste.

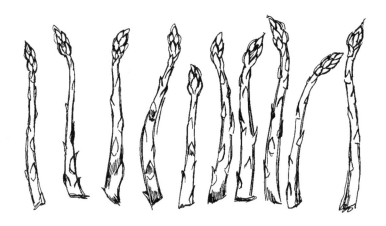

It may feel like cheating to use a curry paste, but if you can find a good-quality one that you like, it can be the key to one of the quickest suppers you will make. With firm pieces of fish, tender sweet potato, sweet cherry tomatoes, and crunchy sugar snap peas all wrapped up in a creamy spicy broth, this makes a hearty and nutritious supper, especially when served with quinoa.

Thai Red Curry

1. While the quinoa is cooking, heat the oil in a separate large pan over medium-high heat and add the shallots and ginger. Fry for 3–4 minutes until softened. Add the curry paste, tomatoes, and sweet potato and stir-fry for a further 2–3 minutes.

2. Pour in the coconut milk and vegetable stock, bring to a boil, and then reduce the heat to a steady simmer and cook for 10–12 minutes, or until the sweet potato is tender. Add the fish sauce, brown sugar, sugar snap peas, and baby corn and simmer for 3 minutes. Squeeze in the lime juice, stir, and taste, adjusting with more fish sauce, sugar, or lime juice, as needed.

3. Add the fish cubes and simmer for 3–5 minutes until just cooked. Stir in some of the basil and cilantro leaves before serving over bowls of quinoa. Garnish with the remaining basil and cilantro leaves.

Serves 4

1⅓ cups cooked quinoa (see page 214)

1 tbsp canola or vegetable oil

2 shallots, peeled and finely sliced

Thumb-size piece of fresh ginger, peeled and finely sliced

3 tbsps Thai red curry paste

1 cup cherry tomatoes

1 large sweet potato, peeled and diced

1 14-oz can light coconut milk

¾ cup vegetable stock

1 tbsp Thai fish sauce (*nam pla*)

1 tsp brown sugar

5 oz sugar snap peas

12 ears baby corn, frozen or jarred (3 pcs per serving)

Juice of 2 limes

1⅓ lbs skinless fish filet, such as cod or haddock, cut into 1-inch cubes

Small handful each of basil and cilantro leaves, roughly torn

The meaty flavor of mushrooms lends itself extremely well to this "orzotto," using pearl barley, a hearty, nutty-flavored grain. To intensify the flavor of this dish, soak some dried porcini mushrooms in boiling water for a few minutes and then add them to the risotto, along with their soaking liquid.

Pearl Barley and Mushroom Risotto

1. Place the dried mushrooms in a bowl and cover with hot water. Allow to soak for 5–10 minutes.

2. Heat 1 teaspoon of the olive oil in a large nonstick frying pan over medium-high heat and add the mixed mushrooms. Fry until just tender, and then stir in the garlic and season to taste. Fry for two more minutes before removing from the heat. Stir in the parsley, reserving a little to garnish. Drain the dried mushrooms, reserving the soaking liquid for later, and stir them into the pan. Transfer the mushroom mixture to a plate and set aside.

3. Heat the remaining oil in the same pan over medium-high heat and sauté the shallots gently for 8 minutes, or until they become soft and sweet. Stir in the thyme and pearl barley and fry gently before adding the wine and cooking for 2 minutes to allow the grains to soak up the flavors in the pan. Pour in just enough stock to cover the pearl barley and then allow it to bubble away, until all the liquid has been absorbed. Repeat this process, adding the stock a little at a time, until the barley is tender and has absorbed all the liquid. (This should take about 35 minutes.)

4. Stir in the pecorino and mushrooms. Taste and adjust the seasoning. If the risotto is too dry, add a splash of boiling water. Serve the risotto in shallow bowls with a sprinkling of parsley, a drizzle of extra-virgin olive oil, and some more grated pecorino.

Serves 4

¾ oz dried mushrooms

3 tbsps olive oil

12 oz mixed mushrooms

2 garlic cloves, finely chopped

Large handful of flat-leaf parsley, roughly chopped

3 shallots, finely chopped

3 thyme sprigs, leaves finely chopped

1½ cups pearl barley

5 tbsps white wine

1 quart vegetable stock

½ cup grated pecorino, plus extra to serve

Sea salt and freshly ground black pepper

Extra-virgin olive oil, to serve

Tequila Chicken Quinoa Mango Salad

I'm a bit of a lightweight when it comes to booze, as my friends like to remind me on a constant basis. I'd sooner use tequila in cooking than down a shot of the stuff! In this recipe, the tequila lends a peppery sharpness to the lime- and mint-infused chicken marinade, which will give you extra tender meat. Paired with a sweet and savory mango quinoa salad, it may almost make you forget your late-night misadventures . . . well, almost.

Serves 4

For the chicken

4 skinless chicken breasts (about 6 oz each)

1 garlic clove

1 green chili

6 tbsps tequila

Zest and juice of 2 limes

1 tsp chili powder

1 tbsp olive oil

Small handful of fresh mint leaves, chopped

Generous pinch of sea salt and freshly ground pepper

Olive oil, for brushing

For the mango salad

1 tsp sugar

Juice of 1 lime

3 tbsps fish sauce (*nam pla*)

1 cup cooked quinoa (see page 214)

1¼ cups bean sprouts

5 scallions, thinly sliced

1 ripe mango, peeled, pitted, and sliced lengthwise

2 heads of Little Gem lettuces, roughly shredded

Handful of peanuts, toasted and chopped

Handful of fresh mint, chopped

Handful of fresh cilantro, chopped

1. Place all the ingredients for the chicken into a resealable bag and shake to combine. Marinate in the fridge for at least 2 hours, ideally overnight, turning once or twice, if you remember.

2. To make the salad, whisk together the sugar, lime juice, and fish sauce in a large bowl until the sugar has completely dissolved. Add the quinoa, bean sprouts, scallions, mango, and the torn lettuce, and toss to combine.

3. Place a large grill pan over medium-high heat and brush lightly with oil. Remove the chicken breasts from the marinade and fry for 4–5 minutes on each side, or until cooked all the way through. Remove from the heat and slice each breast into chunks.

4. Divide the mango quinoa salad among 4 plates and sprinkle each with some chopped peanuts, mint, and cilantro. Top with the chicken slices and serve immediately.

One of my favorite Thai salads is this minced chicken dish (*laab gai*), which is full of fresh flavor from the mint leaves and lime juice. It can also be made with minced pork or a vegetarian alternative.

Thai Minced Chicken Salad

1. Toast the rice in a large, dry frying pan over medium-high heat, until golden brown. Transfer to a mortar and pound the rice with a pestle—you are looking for a rough texture, rather than a fine powder. Set aside.

2. Place the garlic, chili, and ginger in a food processor and process until finely chopped. Add the chicken and pulse until smooth.

3. Heat the sunflower oil in the same frying pan over high heat, add the minced chicken, and fry for 2–3 minutes, breaking up the chicken with a spatula as it cooks. Continue to cook until the chicken is cooked all the way through, browned slightly, and broken into small pieces.

4. Add the fish sauce and sugar and stir together, frying for another minute until you have a good color on the meat. Add half the scallions, the mint, toasted rice, and lime zest and juice and fry for 1–2 minutes, until the scallions are just tender.

5. Arrange the lettuce leaves on two plates and top with the chicken mixture. Garnish with extra mint leaves and remaining scallions. Serve warm.

Serves 2

¼ cup sweet white rice (sticky rice)

3 garlic cloves, finely chopped

1 red chili pepper, deseeded and finely chopped

Thumb-size piece of fresh ginger, peeled

2 large, skinless chicken breasts (about 6 oz each), cut into large chunks

1 tbsp sunflower oil

1 tbsp fish sauce (*nam pla*)

1 tsp sugar

5 scallions, finely chopped

Generous handful of fresh mint leaves, roughly chopped

Zest and juice of 1 lime

2 heads of Little Gem lettuces, leaves separated

Nutty Chicken Satay Salad

As crunchy, creamy, nutty, chicken satay salads go, this one has a lot to offer. Based on one of my favorite Asian street foods, chicken satay, it's got all the best bits—tender chicken in an aromatic peanut sauce, along with a simple crunchy salad. Mix and match the vegetables as you wish, but do choose ones that have a bite to them.

Serves 4

2 large, skinless chicken breasts (about 6 oz each), thinly sliced

1 tbsp turmeric

2 tsps ground coriander

1 tsp ground cumin

2 garlic cloves, finely chopped

Thumb-size piece of fresh ginger, finely chopped

1 tsp sugar

1 tsp canola or vegetable oil

1 zucchini

1 cucumber

2 large carrots

5 scallions, finely sliced on the diagonal

Handful of salted peanuts, roughly chopped

For the peanut satay sauce

1 tsp sunflower oil

1 garlic clove, very finely chopped

Small thumb-size piece of fresh ginger, peeled and very finely chopped

1 small red chili pepper, deseeded and finely chopped

¾ cup light coconut milk

Juice of 1 lime

3 tbsps crunchy peanut butter

½ tbsp dark soy sauce

1. Place the sliced chicken in a large bowl with the turmeric, coriander, cumin, garlic, ginger, and sugar and toss to coat. Marinate for 30 minutes, ideally overnight, if you have time.

2. Heat the oil in a large frying pan over medium-high heat. Fry the chicken for 6–8 minutes, or until cooked all the way through.

3. To make the peanut sauce, heat the oil in a small pan, add the garlic, ginger, and chili, and fry for 30–40 seconds, stirring continuously. Add the coconut milk, lime juice, peanut butter, and soy sauce. Bring to a boil, stirring to melt the peanut butter, then reduce the heat and simmer for 2–3 minutes.

4. Use a vegetable peeler or spiralizer to make long strands of the zucchini, cucumber, and carrots. Place the raw veggie noodles in a large mixing bowl and add most of the scallions, saving a few to use as a garnish. Pour in the peanut sauce and toss all the ingredients together until combined. Serve with the chicken pieces and a sprinkle of chopped peanuts and the reserved scallion slices. Enjoy warm or cold.

Poached Coconut Chicken

A delicate and light chicken dish that is full of exotic flavors. The fresh bite and crunch from the vegetables in the rich coconut sauce works really well.

Serves 2

Zest and juice of 2 limes

Small thumb-size piece of fresh ginger, peeled and chopped

Large handful of cilantro leaves and stems, roughly chopped

2 lemongrass stalks, trimmed and roughly chopped

1 tsp vegetable oil

1 14-oz can light coconut milk

2 large, skinless chicken breasts (about 6 oz each), cut into strips

3 tbsps Thai fish sauce (*nam pla*)

1 tsp sesame oil

8 oz flat rice noodles, cooked

2 heads of bok choy, roughly sliced

1 cucumber, shaved into ribbons (using a vegetable peeler)

2 celery stalks, thinly sliced

1 bunch of scallions, trimmed and thinly sliced on the diagonal

Chopped cilantro, to garnish

1. Use a hand-held stick blender or mini food processor to combine the lime zest, ginger, cilantro, and lemongrass, until you have a smooth paste.

2. Heat the vegetable oil in a large wok over high heat. Add the paste and fry for 1–2 minutes, until it is aromatic. Add the coconut milk and mix together, then stir in the chicken strips and cook over gentle heat for 8 minutes. Add the fish sauce and simmer for another 5 minutes. Add the lime juice and sesame oil and stir. Remove the chicken and slice into bite-size pieces.

3. Warm the cooked noodles by covering them with boiling water. Drain and divide between 2 shallow bowls, then top with the bok choy, cucumber, celery, and chicken pieces. Ladle the hot coconut broth over everything and garnish with sliced scallions and cilantro leaves.

Chicken Schnitzel with Little Gem and Pea Caesar

A perfectly cooked chicken schnitzel is a beautiful thing, particularly when it is served with my simplified version of a Caesar salad. I like to make this with the first of my own home-grown garden peas, which are so sweet, they can be eaten raw.

Serves 2

2 large, skinless chicken breasts (about 5 oz each)

2 cups breadcrumbs (preferably sourdough)

3 tbsps freshly grated Parmesan

1 tbsp freshly chopped flat-leaf parsley

1 free-range egg

2 tbsps milk

3 tbsps seasoned flour

3 tbsps vegetable oil

4 heads of Little Gem lettuces, trimmed and quartered

½ cup freshly shelled peas

For the Caesar dressing

1 medium free-range egg

2 anchovy filets (from a jar or can)

Few drops of Worcestershire sauce

1 tsp lemon juice

½ cup vegetable oil

Sea salt and freshly ground black pepper

1. First make the Caesar dressing. Put the egg, anchovy filets, Worcestershire sauce, and lemon juice in a mini food processor and process until just combined. With the motor running, gradually add the vegetable oil and process until thick and creamy. Season with salt and pepper, and add a little water if you find the dressing a little thick.

2. Slice each chicken breast in half and then flatten the pieces slightly by placing them between 2 sheets of plastic wrap and using a rolling pin to make thin cutlets. Place the breadcrumbs in a bowl with the Parmesan and parsley. Beat the egg and milk together in a separate bowl. Dust the chicken cutlets in the seasoned flour, then dip them in the beaten egg mixture and coat with the breadcrumbs.

3. Place a large, nonstick frying pan over medium-high heat. When the pan is hot, add the vegetable oil and then add the coated chicken cutlets. Cook for 2–3 minutes on each side, turning once, until the chicken is cooked through and the Parmesan crumbs are golden. Drain on paper towels.

4. Arrange the Little Gem lettuce, cut sides up, on each plate and scatter the peas on top. Drizzle the Caesar dressing over the salad, and then add a chicken schnitzel to each plate to serve.

time
for
dinner

Time to get down to business! Fresh and light dinners require some new thinking, an injection of vegetables, some exciting cooking methods, a little less meat, and when you do cook with it, meat of higher quality. My main aim with lighter meals is to not compromise on flavor; instead I put it front and center of each dish. In these recipes I rely on cooking methods like roasting, which brings out the natural sweetness of vegetables, zingy and tangy dressings and salsas to add a final punch to dishes, and electric spice mixes to take fish, chicken, grains, and more to another level. And—most importantly—I focus on contrasting textures: crunchy and silky, crisp and chewy. All these elements are bound to leave you with some seriously FRESH dishes.

There are quite a few vegetable-centric recipes in this chapter for healthy evening meals that don't skimp on the flavor front, like Roasted Squash Salad with Sriracha Yogurt (and cilantro salsa), Mediterranean Vegetable Tart (with a slightly controversial— and surprisingly terrific!) goat cheese cauliflower crust, a completely meat-free Super Power Chili with Charred Corn Salsa that has all the extra elements you have come to expect, and the brilliant, blushing Mega Beet Burgers, which look just as good as they taste! On the non-vegetarian front, there are also dishes to delight in, like Spiced Fish with Mango Salsa and Brown Rice Salad, and Pomegranate Molasses Chicken, my new way to roast chicken, served with roasted vegetables that have been tossed with bulgur wheat—a perfect one-pot dish. These are recipes to get excited about! There are also four great side dishes to choose among, and that would also sit happily alongside many of the recipes in this chapter. And I can never speak highly enough of the humble salad: a bowl of simple dressed greens is always a welcome addition and will boost your intake of greens. Time to eat!

Roast Chickpea, Carrot, Mint, and Halloumi Salad

I am slightly addicted to halloumi cheese; its saltiness and unique texture, and the fact that it can be fried, make it a great alternative to meat in a salad like this. Roasting chickpeas gives them an altogether different texture, slightly crispy on the outside, and makes them perfect for adding to salads or just as a simple snack.

Serves 4

1 14-oz can chickpeas, drained and rinsed

2 cups tomatoes, halved

2 tsps vegetable oil, plus extra for frying

1 tsp smoked paprika

7 oz halloumi cheese, cut into ½-inch-thick slices

1 Little Gem lettuce, leaves separated

2 large carrots, julienned

½ red onion, thinly sliced

Sea salt and freshly ground black pepper

For the dressing

3 tbsps extra-virgin olive oil

1 tbsp lemon juice

1 tbsp cider vinegar

1 tsp Dijon mustard

1 garlic clove, very finely chopped

1. Preheat the oven to 400°F (350°F fan).

2. Place the chickpeas and tomatoes in a roasting pan and drizzle with the oil. Season with salt and pepper and sprinkle with the paprika; toss to coat. Roast in the oven for about 35 minutes, or until the tomatoes have shrunk and become caramelized.

3. Whisk together all the ingredients for the dressing in a large mixing bowl and set aside.

4. Heat a little vegetable oil in a large frying pan over medium-high heat and add the halloumi slices. Season with salt and pepper while the slices are in the pan and fry on both sides until they are golden brown. Remove from the pan and set aside.

5. Add the Little Gem leaves, carrots, red onion, tomatoes, and chickpeas to the bowl of dressing and mix until all the ingredients are coated.

6. Pile the salad onto plates and top with the slices of halloumi.

Pumpkins and squash are two of my favorite vegetables to grow. There are so many incredible varieties, shapes, and sizes, and I love the way they grow with vigor through the summer months, from floppy golden flowers into tough orbs ready for autumn. Roasting them brings out their sweetness and makes them a meaty main ingredient that's ideal for a salad like this one, laced with a vibrant and sharp aromatic cilantro salsa.

Roasted Squash Salad with Sriracha Yogurt

1. Preheat the oven to 400°F (350°F fan).

2. Place the squash and red onion quarters into a large roasting pan and drizzle with oil. Sprinkle the cumin, chili flakes, and smoked paprika on top, and mix until completely coated. Roast in the oven for 45 minutes, or until the squash is tender and slightly caramelized.

3. For the salsa, blend the oil, cilantro, chili, lime zest and juice, and salt together in a food processor until completely combined. Set aside. Prepare the sriracha yogurt by stirring together the yogurt and hot sauce. Season with salt and pepper and set aside.

4. Mix together the fennel, lentils, and chickpeas in a large bowl and then stir in half the cilantro salsa.

5. Divide the fennel, lentil, and chickpea mixture among 4 plates and top with the roasted squash and onions. Add a dollop of sriracha yogurt and the remaining cilantro salsa. Finally, garnish with cilantro leaves.

Serves 4

2 small butternut squash, peeled and cut into wedges

2 small red onions, quartered with the root left intact

1 tbsp vegetable oil

1 tsp ground cumin

1 tsp red chili flakes

1 tsp smoked paprika

2 fennel bulbs, thinly sliced

1 14-oz can green lentils, drained and rinsed

1 14-oz can chickpeas, drained and rinsed

For the cilantro salsa

2 tbsps extra-virgin olive oil

Large handful of cilantro, plus extra to garnish

1 green chili, finely chopped

Zest and juice of 1 lime

Sea salt

For the sriracha yogurt

6 tbsps plain yogurt

1 tsp sriracha hot sauce

Sea salt and freshly ground black pepper

Squash, Spinach, and Chickpea Filo Pie

This filo pie would make a fantastic vegetarian centerpiece at a dinner party, but it would also be delicious, taken warm from the oven, on a picnic. Remember to cover unused sheets of filo with a damp dish towel as you work to keep them from drying out.

Serves 6

4 tbsps vegetable oil

1 small onion, diced

1 large garlic clove, finely chopped

1 heaping tsp grated fresh ginger

1 tsp garam masala

½ tsp each of ground cumin and coriander

1 lb sweet potatoes, peeled and diced

1 14-oz can chickpeas, drained and rinsed

¾ cup vegetable stock

1 14-oz can chopped tomatoes

½ cup light coconut milk

Good pinch of sugar (optional)

⅔ cup frozen spinach

8–10 filo pastry sheets, thawed if frozen

Sea salt and freshly ground black pepper

Lightly dressed mixed green salad, to serve

1. Heat 1 tablespoon of the vegetable oil in a large, heavy-bottom pan and sauté the onion until softened and just beginning to brown around the edges. Stir in the garlic and ginger and cook for another 30 seconds or so. Add the spices and cook for another minute, stirring.

2. Add the sweet potatoes and chickpeas to the pan and mix well to combine, then sauté them for a couple of minutes. Stir in the stock, tomatoes, coconut milk, and sugar, if using. Season with salt and pepper. Bring to a boil, then reduce the heat and simmer for about 15 minutes, or until the sweet potatoes are completely tender but still hold their shape.

3. Fold the spinach into the sweet potato mixture and cook for another couple of minutes until the spinach is cooked through and tender. The mixture should be nice and chunky at this point—any excess liquid should have been reduced. Remove the mixture from the heat and let cool completely.

4. Preheat the oven to 350°F (325°F fan). Brush the base and sides of a large 1½-quart ovenproof frying pan with vegetable oil (or you can use a 9-inch removable-bottom cake pan).

5. Brush 4–6 of the filo sheets with vegetable oil, then lay them in the bottom of the pan so they drape over the sides. Spoon in the cooled sweet potato mixture and spread it out over the bottom of the pan. Fold the overhanging pastry over the top to cover the filling. Scrunch the remaining filo sheets and arrange on top to cover the top of the pie (you may not need all of them), brushing with a little extra oil. Bake for 25–30 minutes, or until the filo is crisp and golden.

6. If using a frying pan, carefully slide the pie onto a board (or remove it from the pan). Cut into slices and serve with green salad.

Squash Tagine with Quinoa

Although I own a traditional tagine, it rarely makes an appearance when I cook this dish, as I tend to use a deep frying pan, which does the job perfectly. Instead, my poor conical tagine is relegated to the bottom shelf of my cupboard, where it sits, judged by all the regular kitchenware and jealous of their ability to stack correctly. Whatever you choose to cook this recipe in, you are in for a treat. It's a stunning medley of sweet, vitamin-packed vegetables in a subtly spiced tomato sauce bursting with jewels of dried fruit.

Serves 4

⅓ cup dried apricots, finely sliced

⅓ cup golden raisins

1 tsp ground ginger

1 tsp freshly ground black pepper

1 tsp ground turmeric

1 tsp cayenne pepper

2 tsps smoked paprika

1 tbsp vegetable oil

2 onions, roughly chopped

8 garlic cloves, finely chopped

1 butternut squash, peeled and cut into bite-size pieces

2 large carrots, cut into bite-size pieces

1 zucchini, cut into bite-size pieces

1 tbsp honey

2 14-oz cans chopped tomatoes

½ tbsp vegetable bouillon powder

1 14-oz can chickpeas, drained and rinsed

1½ cups quinoa (see page 214)

Handful of toasted sliced almonds, plus extra to serve

Handful of fresh cilantro, roughly chopped, plus extra to serve

1. Place the apricots and raisins in small bowl and pour just enough boiling water to cover them. Combine all the ground spices together in a bowl.

2. Heat the oil in a large, deep frying pan over medium heat. Add the onions and garlic and fry for 4 minutes, then stir in the spice mixture and fry gently until the onions are soft.

3. Add the butternut squash, carrots, and zucchini and fry for 3–4 minutes, tossing to coat everything in the spices. Add the apricots and raisins (and their soaking liquid), honey, chopped tomatoes, and bouillon powder. Bring to a boil, then reduce the heat and simmer for 15–20 minutes, or until the carrots are just tender. Add the drained chickpeas and allow to heat through for a few minutes.

4. Cook the quinoa and then stir in the toasted almonds and chopped cilantro. Serve the tagine on top of the quinoa, sprinkled generously with more toasted almonds and cilantro.

A noodle dish like this one is all about textures: silky rice noodles and tofu, tender vegetables with a little bite, and the crunch of bean sprouts and peanuts, all combined with aromatic herbs and a sweet and spicy sauce. It makes a delicious dinner, but I often use any leftovers as a great lunch-box filler the following day.

Lemongrass and Ginger Nutty Tofu Noodles

1. Place the tofu in a bowl with the garlic, lemongrass, chili, and ginger. Cover and marinate in the fridge for at least 30 minutes.

2. Soak the noodles in a bowl of boiling water for 6 minutes (or according to the instructions on the package). Drain and set aside.

3. Heat the oil in a wok over high heat and swirl to coat the sides. Add the celery, carrot, red pepper, and scallions. Stir-fry for 5 minutes until softened. Remove from the pan with a slotted spoon and set aside on a plate.

4. Return the wok to the heat with an extra drizzle of oil, if needed. Fry the marinated tofu until golden on all sides. Return the vegetables to the pan and toss with the curry powder, sugar, and vegetable stock. Simmer for 5–6 minutes until the liquid has reduced slightly.

5. Add the noodles, bean sprouts, and herbs. Toss everything together until it's well combined. Serve sprinkled with handfuls of chopped peanuts and herbs.

Serves 4

12 oz firm tofu, cut into bite-size pieces

3 garlic cloves, very finely chopped

2 lemongrass stalks, finely chopped

1 red chili, deseeded and finely chopped

Thumb-size piece of fresh ginger, peeled and grated

4 oz flat rice noodles

1 tbsp sunflower oil, plus extra if needed

2 celery stalks, finely sliced

1 carrot, julienned

1 red pepper, deseeded and finely sliced

4 scallions, cut into 1-inch batons

1 tbsp curry powder

1 tbsp sugar

7 tbsps vegetable stock

Large handful of bean sprouts

Small handful each of mint, basil, and cilantro leaves, plus extra to garnish

Large handful of peanuts, roughly chopped

Most people have come across the mighty Pad Thai, but its lesser-known cousin, the humorously titled Pad Prik, is also certainly worth a look. Essentially a dry curry with green beans and whatever protein you choose, it makes for a simple and quick supper. I've added vitamin-C-rich peppers to the mix—feel free to add whatever vegetables you see fit, once you've figured out the basic method. Tofu can be found in most supermarkets, but try looking for it in Asian supermarkets, where you should also be able to get your hands on kaffir lime leaves.

Tofu Pad Prik

1. Heat the vegetable oil in a large wok over medium-high heat. Add the tofu and fry until it is golden brown on all sides. Remove from the wok with a slotted spoon and drain on paper towels; set aside.

2. Add the red curry paste to the wok and fry for 2 minutes, until it becomes aromatic. Add the green beans and peppers, and fry until the vegetables are tender.

3. Return the tofu to the wok and then pour in the vegetable stock, fish sauce, and sugar, if using. Simmer for 5 minutes, until the sauce has reduced slightly.

4. Remove from the heat and add the kaffir lime leaves, stirring to combine. Serve with brown rice and top with the torn basil leaves and toasted peanuts.

Serves 4

1 tbsp vegetable oil

9 oz firm tofu, cut into 1-inch squares

4 tbsps Thai red curry paste

About 2 cups green beans, trimmed

1 red pepper, deseeded and cut into 1-inch squares

1 green pepper, deseeded and cut into 1-inch squares

5 tbsps vegetable stock

1 tbsp fish sauce (*nam pla*)

½ tsp sugar (optional)

6 fresh kaffir lime leaves, finely sliced

1⅓ cups cooked brown rice, to serve

Large handful of Thai basil leaves, torn

Large handful of peanuts, toasted

Roast Cabbage with Carrot Purée and Fried Halloumi

I'm sure you've been in the situation of having nothing in the house, but dinner still needs to be on the table, regardless! A quick rummage in the kitchen more often than not results in some decent bounty. This dish is one I came up with in that exact situation. The vegetables are transformed by roasting, and the addition of a vibrant spice and a silky-sweet purée makes a surprisingly delicious supper.

Serves 4

1 head of napa cabbage, quartered

1¼ lbs Brussels sprouts, trimmed and halved (about 5½ cups)

1 head of cauliflower, cut into florets

1 red onion, thickly sliced but root left intact

Olive oil, for drizzling

½ tsp cayenne pepper

1 tsp smoked paprika

3 large carrots, diced

1 roasted red pepper (from a jar), drained and roughly chopped

3 tbsps plain yogurt

1 tsp vegetable oil

4 oz halloumi, sliced

Sea salt

1. Preheat the oven to 400°F (350°F fan).

2. Place the cabbage, Brussels sprouts, cauliflower, and red onion on a large baking tray in a single layer. (Use two baking sheets if necessary; it's fairly essential you don't overcrowd the tray, otherwise the vegetables will sweat.) Drizzle with olive oil and sprinkle with cayenne pepper, paprika, and sea salt.

3. Place the tray in the oven to roast for about 40 minutes, or until the vegetables are tender and slightly charred.

4. While the vegetables cook, steam the carrots until they are tender. Transfer to a food processor, along with the roasted red pepper, yogurt, and a sprinkle of sea salt. Process until you have a smooth purée.

5. Heat the vegetable oil in a frying pan over medium–high heat and fry the halloumi slices until golden.

6. Spread each plate with a dollop of the carrot purée and top with the roasted vegetables and fried halloumi slices. Serve immediately.

Mediterranean Vegetable Tart with Goat Cheese Cauliflower Crust

This delicious tart uses a cauliflower crust, which is a really wonderful healthy alternative to pastry. The crust can also be used as a gluten-free pizza base.

Serves 4

6 oz eggplant, cut into bite-size pieces (about 1 small eggplant)

1 small zucchini, cut into bite-size pieces

1 red onion, cut into bite-size pieces

1 red pepper, deseeded and cut into bite-size pieces

2 tbsps olive oil

Pinch of crushed dried chilies (optional)

Sea salt and freshly ground black pepper

For the goat cheese cauliflower crust

1 head of cauliflower (about 1¼ lbs), broken into florets

1 large free-range egg

5 oz goat cheese

1 tsp dried oregano

Small handful of basil, roughly chopped, plus extra to garnish

Sea salt and freshly ground black pepper

1. Preheat the oven to 400°F (350°F fan).

2. To make the crust, place the cauliflower florets in a food processor. Process until you have an extremely fine consistency, almost like fluffed-up couscous. Pile the cauliflower onto a large thin dish towel, wrap up, and squeeze out as much liquid as you can.

3. Transfer the dry cauliflower to a mixing bowl and add the egg, 3½ oz of the goat cheese, oregano, basil, and salt and pepper. Mix well to combine; when it starts to stick together, transfer the mixture to a baking sheet lined with parchment paper. Press it out to form a rough oval, about ⅓-inch thick, leaving the edges a little thicker for the crust. Place on the top rack of the oven and bake for 40–45 minutes, or until golden brown.

4. Put all the prepared vegetables into a large, nonstick, shallow roasting pan, making sure you don't overcrowd it. Drizzle with olive oil, season with salt and pepper, and toss to coat.

5. Roast the vegetables on the middle rack of the oven for about 30 minutes, or until the vegetables are cooked through, but haven't yet become scorched around the edges. Remove the pan from the oven and allow to cool slightly.

6. When both the vegetables and crust are cooked, spoon the roasted vegetables over the crust, sprinkle with chili flakes, if using, and spoon on dollops of the remaining goat cheese. Bake for 10–15 minutes. Sprinkle the remaining basil leaves on top, cut into slices, and serve.

These light but zesty cakes can be used in salads, wraps, and lunch boxes, so it is a good idea to make two batches, as they freeze extremely well. I serve them with a vibrant, minty salsa verde, a classic Italian sauce that complements the zucchini and peas. Serve it with a lightly dressed arugula salad, and it makes a light lunch or a robust appetizer.

Mini Quinoa, Pea, and Zucchini Cakes

1. Preheat the oven to 400°F (350°F fan).

2. Heat the vegetable oil in a large frying pan over medium-high heat and fry the garlic and onion for 4–5 minutes, or until softened. Add the zucchini and fry for a further 5 minutes until softened. Just before the zucchini is cooked, add the peas and stir. Set the cooked vegetables aside to cool completely in a large mixing bowl.

3. In a food processor blend together the pumpkin seeds and flax seeds until they are finely ground. Add the chickpeas, lemon zest and juice, and blend again until smooth.

4. Transfer the mixture to the cooked vegetables in the bowl, along with the scallions, cooked quinoa, basil, and mint. Season with salt and pepper and mix until all the ingredients are evenly combined. If the mixture looks too dry, loosen with 1–2 tablespoons of cold water.

5. Using your hands, form the mixture into golf ball–size balls and then press into ¼-inch-thick patties. Place on a baking sheet lined with parchment paper and bake for 25 minutes, or until golden brown.

6. Blend all the ingredients for the salsa verde in a food processor until smooth. Transfer to individual serving dishes.

7. Dress the arugula with a squeeze of lemon juice, a drizzle of extra-virgin olive oil, and some salt and pepper; toss to coat. Serve the mini cakes with the salsa verde and dressed arugula.

Serves 6

1 tbsp vegetable oil

2 garlic cloves, very finely chopped

1 onion, finely chopped

2 zucchini, coarsely grated

¾ cup frozen peas, defrosted

6 tbsps pumpkin seeds

3 tbsps flax seeds

1 14-oz can chickpeas, drained and rinsed

Zest and juice of ½ lemon

3 scallions, finely sliced

1 cup cooked quinoa (see page 214)

Small handful of basil, chopped

Small handful of mint, chopped

Sea salt and freshly ground black pepper

For the salsa verde

6 tbsps extra-virgin olive oil, plus extra for dressing the salad

2 tbsps red wine vinegar

1 tsp Dijon mustard

2 garlic cloves

3 anchovy filets

1 tbsp capers, drained and rinsed

Handful of flat-leaf parsley

Large handful of mint leaves

½ tsp salt

½ tsp pepper

To serve

3 large handfuls of arugula

½ lemon

Super Power Chili with Charred Corn Salsa

Making a meatless chili con carne is surprisingly simple; replacing beef or pork with grains like lentils and quinoa makes for a deliciously light, yet rich and filling meal. You might be thinking it's not going to fool you or the meat eater in your life, but I promise, when you serve it up with a spicy smoky corn salsa and all the other accompaniments, nobody will have any complaints!

Serves 4–6

1 tbsp coconut oil

1 large onion, finely diced

1 carrot, finely diced

1 celery stalk, finely diced

Large thumb-size piece of fresh ginger, peeled and finely chopped

3 garlic cloves, very finely chopped

1 red chili pepper, finely chopped

1 tbsp coriander seeds, toasted and ground

1 tbsp cumin seeds, toasted and ground

1 tbsp chili powder

1 tsp smoked paprika

1½ cups quinoa, uncooked

1¼ cups green lentils

2 14-oz cans plum tomatoes

1 quart vegetable stock

1 14-oz can kidney beans, drained and rinsed

Sea salt and freshly ground black pepper

For the smoky corn salsa

2 ears of corn

1 tsp coconut oil

2 tbsps cilantro, finely chopped

1 tsp smoky Tabasco sauce

To serve

2 ripe avocados, peeled and pitted and thinly sliced

Large handful of cilantro

2 limes, cut into wedges

Plain yogurt (optional)

1. Melt the coconut oil in a large casserole over medium-high heat. Add the onion, carrot, celery, and ginger and fry for 4–5 minutes, until just tender. Stir in the garlic, red chlli pepper, coriander and cumin seeds, chili powder, and paprika and fry for a further 2–3 minutes.

2. Add the quinoa, lentils, plum tomatoes, and vegetable stock and bring to a boil. Reduce the heat, season with salt and pepper, and simmer gently for 45 minutes, or until the grains are tender and cooked through. Keep adding liquid, if needed, until the grains are tender.

3. Add the kidney beans and cook for 5 more minutes. Taste and adjust the seasoning and cover with a lid until ready to serve.

4. While the chili is cooking, prepare the corn salsa. Boil the corn in a pot of water for 8–10 minutes, or until tender. Slice the cooked corn kernels off the cobs. Heat a large frying pan over high heat. Add the coconut oil and fry the corn kernels, without stirring, until slightly charred. Stir in the chopped cilantro and Tabasco, and season generously with salt and pepper.

5. Serve the chili in deep bowls, topped with avocado slices, spoonfuls of corn salsa, cilantro, lime wedges, and a dollop of yogurt, if using.

Mega Beet Burgers

Beets are easy enough to grow, and there is a huge selection of varieties and colors to choose from, such as pale pinks, candy-striped, and even golden yellow. These vegetarian burgers are a great way of showing them off.

Makes 6 burgers

3 tbsps olive oil

1 red onion, finely chopped

2 garlic cloves, crushed

2 raw beets, peeled and grated

1 zucchini, grated

2 large carrots, grated

1 heaping cup rolled oats

1 14-oz can chickpeas, drained and rinsed

3 tbsps tahini

1 large free-range egg

4 scallions, finely sliced

3 tbsps chopped cilantro

Sea salt and freshly ground black pepper

To serve

Whole wheat sourdough buns, split and toasted

Chickpea Hummus (see page 27)

Avocado slices

Bean sprouts

Shredded red cabbage

1. Heat about 1 tablespoon of the oil in a large frying pan over medium heat. Sauté the onion and garlic for 4–5 minutes or until softened. Add the grated vegetables and cook, stirring, for about 5 minutes until softened, then drain off any liquid.

2. Place the oats, chickpeas, tahini, and egg in a food processor and pulse to combine. Transfer the mixture to a bowl, stir in the cooked vegetables, scallions, and cilantro, and season generously with salt and pepper.

3. Form the mixture into 6 burgers and chill for about 30 minutes (or up to 24 hours). Heat the remaining oil in a nonstick frying pan over medium heat and cook the burgers, in batches if necessary, for about 2–3 minutes on each side, until golden.

4. Serve the burgers on toasted sourdough buns with the hummus, avocado, bean sprouts, and red cabbage.

Roasted Sweet Potato 4 Ways

Indian

Serves 4

4 large sweet potatoes (about 1¼ lbs)

1 tbsp vegetable oil

½ cup plain yogurt

1 tsp curry powder

1 garlic clove, peeled and very finely chopped

1 red chili pepper, deseeded, if you wish, and finely sliced diagonally

Large handful of cilantro leaves

1. Preheat the oven to 400°F (350°F fan). Place the sweet potatoes on a baking tray and drizzle with the oil. Bake in the oven for 45 minutes, or until tender when pierced with a fork.

2. Slice open the baked sweet potatoes to reveal the flesh. Mix the yogurt with the curry powder and garlic, and spoon a generous dollop onto each sweet potato. Sprinkle with the red chili pepper and some roughly torn cilantro leaves.

Mushroom and Spinach

Serves 4

4 large sweet potatoes (about 1¼ lbs)

1½ tbsps vegetable oil

7 oz forest mushrooms (about 2 cups), such as shiitake and oyster, sliced or roughly torn

1 garlic clove, very finely chopped

4 cups spinach leaves

Large handful of parsley, roughly chopped

Sea salt and freshly ground black pepper

1. Preheat the oven to 400°F (350°F fan). Place the sweet potatoes on a baking tray and drizzle with about a tablespoon of oil. Bake in the oven for 45 minutes, or until tender when pierced with a fork.

2. Heat the remaining oil in a frying pan over medium heat and fry the mushrooms until tender. Stir in the garlic, season, and fry 1–2 minutes. Add the spinach and stir until wilted. Mix in the parsley. Slice open the sweet potatoes to reveal the flesh. Top with the mushrooms and spinach.

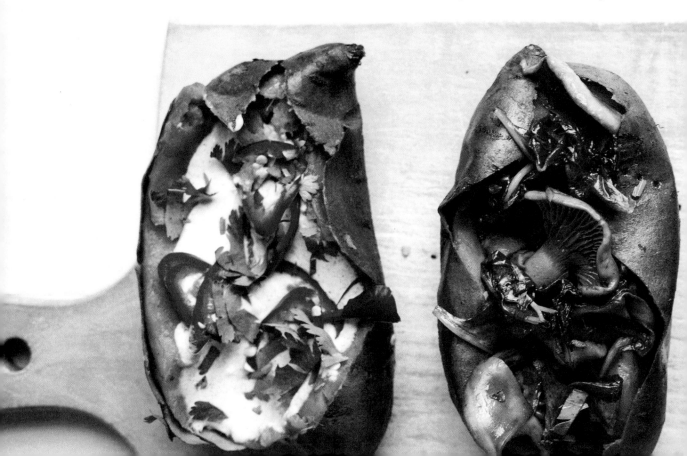

My one healthy-eating saving grace when there is very little in the house, is a roasted sweet potato. Although not exactly fast food, it's worth the wait!

Mexican

Serves 4

4 large sweet potatoes (about 1¼ lbs)

1 tbsp vegetable oil

8 tbsps plain yogurt

8 tbsps salsa

1 ripe avocado, peeled and pitted and thinly sliced

Small handful of tortilla chips (about 2 oz)

Small handful of cilantro leaves

1. Preheat the oven to 400°F (350°F fan). Place the sweet potatoes on a baking tray and drizzle with the oil. Bake in the oven for 45 minutes, or until tender when pierced with a fork.

2. Slice open the baked sweet potatoes to reveal the flesh. Top each with a dollop of yogurt, the salsa, sliced avocado, crunched up tortilla chips, and cilantro leaves.

Superseed and Sprouts

Serves 4

4 large sweet potatoes (about 1¼ lbs)

1½ tbsps vegetable oil

½ bunch kale, leaves torn from the stem

1 garlic clove, finely minced

½ tsp chili flakes

8 tbsps natural probiotic yogurt

1 tbsp pumpkin seeds, toasted

Small handful of alfalfa sprouts (about 2 oz)

Sea salt and freshly ground black pepper

1. Preheat the oven to 400°F (350°F fan). Place the sweet potatoes on a baking tray and drizzle with about a tablespoon of oil. Bake in the oven for 45 minutes, or until tender when pierced with a fork.

2. Heat the remaining oil in a frying pan over medium heat. Add the kale and fry 3−4 minutes, until wilted. Stir in the garlic and chili flakes, and season. Slice open the sweet potatoes. Top with the kale, yogurt, pumpkin seeds, and alfalfa sprouts.

Sweet Potato Shepherdless Pie

The many shepherd's pies I ate during my childhood have nothing on this vegetarian version, which is packed with nutrient-filled ingredients like spinach, sweet potato, and quinoa. Coconut oil is the trendy new health ingredient, but, fads aside, I use it for its exotic sweet flavor and the silky texture it lends to the sweet potato mash.

Serves 4

1 tbsp coconut oil

1 large onion, finely diced

1 large carrot, finely diced

1 celery stalk, finely diced

1 garlic clove, very finely chopped

3 thyme sprigs, leaves only

1¼ lbs mushrooms, roughly chopped

5 tbsps red wine

2 cups vegetable stock

1½ cups quinoa, uncooked

2 14-oz cans green lentils, drained and rinsed

6 cups spinach

Sea salt and freshly ground black pepper

For the topping

2 large sweet potatoes, peeled and diced

1 tbsp coconut oil

2 red onions, finely sliced

1. Melt the coconut oil in a large pan over medium-high heat. Add the onion, carrot, celery, garlic, and thyme and cook for 4–5 minutes, or until softened. Add the mushrooms and cook for 2–3 more minutes. Season with salt and pepper.

2. Pour in the wine, vegetable stock, quinoa, and lentils and simmer for 15 minutes until reduced. Stir in the spinach until just wilted. Taste and adjust the seasoning.

3. Meanwhile, prepare the topping. Steam the sweet potatoes until they are tender and can be pierced easily with a fork.

4. Melt half the coconut oil in a frying pan over medium-high heat and add the red onions. Turn the heat down low, season with salt and pepper, and cook gently, stirring occasionally until softened and caramelized, about 8–10 minutes. Set aside. Preheat the oven to 400°F (350°F fan).

5. Place the sweet potatoes in a bowl with the remaining coconut oil and mash until smooth. Season to taste and then stir in the caramelized red onions.

6. Transfer the lentil mixture to an ovenproof baking dish. Add the sweet potato mash over the top in dollops and spread out evenly across the pie. Place in the oven and cook for 25 minutes until lightly golden. Serve warm from the oven with a green salad.

An authentic dal is hard to beat. The balance of spices is important, so it's worth checking your pantry to see what you have. Store spices in airtight containers away from direct sunlight, and try to use them within three months, as they will start to lose their flavor. This dal would be delicious with a simple piece of steamed fish, but I love a bowl of it just on its own.

Spiced Indian Dal

1. Put the lentils into a heavy-bottom pan with the ginger, cilantro, and salt, then pour in the coconut milk and 2½ cups of water. Bring to a gentle simmer and cook for 30 minutes, stirring frequently, adding the tomatoes after 10 minutes.

2. After 30 minutes the lentils will have broken down and will be thick and creamy. Whisk until the mixture becomes smooth. If it is too thick, you can add a little more water. Leave to simmer gently while you get the spice mixture ready.

3. Heat the oil in a small, heavy-bottom frying pan. Add the turmeric, cumin, coriander, mustard seeds, red chili pepper, and curry leaves to the hot oil—this is known as tempering, when the hot oil brings out the aroma and flavor of the spices. After 30 seconds to 1 minute the mustard seeds should start popping; at this point stir the tempered spices into the lentils, reserving 1 tablespoon. Be careful, as the mixture may spit a little. Whisk until well combined and then stir in the baby spinach, lemon juice, and sliced scallions, reserving a few for the garnish.

4. Ladle the dal into bowls, then sprinkle the cilantro, reserved tempered spices, and scallions on top.

Serves 4

½ cup red lentils

1 tsp grated fresh ginger

Handful of cilantro, finely chopped

1 tsp salt

1 14-oz can light coconut milk

1 14-oz can chopped tomatoes

3 tbsps sunflower oil

1 tsp ground turmeric

½ tsp ground cumin

½ tsp ground coriander

½ tsp mustard seeds

1 red chili pepper, deseeded and finely chopped

8 curry leaves (ideally fresh, but dried is okay)

4 cups baby spinach leaves

Juice of 1 lemon

2 scallions, finely sliced

Cilantro, to garnish

I regularly make this spicy charred fish as the filling for fish tacos. Combined with a cooling sweet mango salsa and a fresh-tasting brown rice salad, it becomes a hearty yet fresh dinner. Most of the elements can be prepared in advance, but only cook the fish when you are ready to serve.

Spiced Fish with Mango Salsa and Brown Rice Salad

Serves 4

1 tbsp smoked paprika

1 tsp garlic powder

1 tsp dried oregano

1 tsp cayenne pepper

1 tsp ground cumin

1½ lbs skinless cod filet

1 tbsp sunflower oil

1. Make the brown rice salad. Allow the cooked rice to cool. Meanwhile, whisk together the garlic, olive oil, and balsamic vinegar in a large bowl. Add the cooled rice, chickpeas, asparagus, parsley, and arugula, and mix until everything is evenly combined. Season with salt and pepper.

2. Make the mango salsa. Cut the cucumber in half lengthwise and use a teaspoon to scoop out and discard the seeds in the middle. Cut the cucumber into dice and add to a bowl with the remaining salsa ingredients (except the cilantro). Season with salt and pepper and stir well to combine, adding the cilantro just before serving.

3. Combine all the ground spices in a bowl, and then use the spice mix to dust the fish filet.

4. Heat a grill pan to medium-high heat. When hot, brush the pan with the sunflower oil and cook the fish for 4–5 minutes on each side until cooked through. (The flesh should be just opaque.) Use a couple of forks to break the fish into large chunks. Serve immediately with the brown rice salad and mango salsa.

For the brown rice salad

1¼ cups cooked brown basmati rice

1 garlic clove, finely chopped

3 tbsps extra-virgin olive oil

1 tbsp balsamic vinegar

1 14-oz can chickpeas, drained, rinsed, and roughly chopped

6 raw or blanched asparagus spears, finely sliced

Large handful of fresh flat-leaf parsley, chopped

4 cups arugula leaves, roughly chopped

Sea salt and freshly ground black pepper

For the mango salsa

½ cucumber

2 mangoes, peeled, pitted, and chopped

4 scallions, trimmed and chopped

1 small red chili pepper, deseeded and chopped

Juice of 1 lime

2 tbsps olive oil

Large handful of cilantro, chopped

Sea salt and freshly ground black pepper

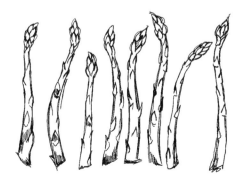

Crispy Spiced Squid with Avocado Salad

This has to be one of the most delicious salads I've ever tasted. It packs a powerful flavor punch that you'll find yourself craving. . . . You have been warned!

Serves 4–6

For the salad

3 firm ripe avocados

1 small red onion, finely sliced

1 cup cherry plum tomatoes, halved

Small handful of fresh cilantro, finely chopped

Juice of 2 limes

2 heads of Little Gem lettuces, outer leaves discarded and separated into leaves

Salt and freshly ground black pepper

For the crispy squid

1 lb medium-size squid, cleaned

2 tbsps cornstarch

3 tbsps semolina

1 tsp smoked paprika

1 tsp sea salt

Sunflower oil for deep-frying

1 red chili pepper, thinly sliced, to garnish

2 scallions, thinly sliced, to garnish

1. Cut the avocados in half and remove the pits, then scoop out the flesh and slice thinly. Place in a bowl with the red onion, cherry plum tomatoes, cilantro, and lime juice. Season with salt and pepper, and gently fold everything together.

2. Scatter the Little Gem lettuce leaves over serving plates and then sprinkle the avocado and tomato mixture on top. Set aside until needed.

3. Cut open the body pouch of each squid along one side, and use a sharp knife to score the inner side into a fine diamond pattern. Then cut each pouch in half lengthwise, then across into 2-inch pieces. Separate the tentacles into pairs.

4. Put the cornstarch, semolina, paprika, and a teaspoon of salt into a resealable bag. Add the prepared squid and then toss to coat. Transfer the squid to a tray, tapping to remove any excess, and leave for 1–2 minutes so that the cornstarch mixture becomes slightly damp. (This will give a crispier finish.)

5. Heat the oil in a deep fryer or large pan to 375°F. Fry the squid in batches for 1–2 minutes. To ensure maximum golden crunchiness don't overcrowd the pan. Drain the squid on paper towels and keep warm.

6. Arrange the crispy squid on top of the salad and garnish with the chili pepper and scallions.

This is a great way to jazz up a traditional Sunday roast—here a whole chicken is marinated in yogurt and spices, making it meltingly tender. The fantastic flavors really penetrate the flesh of the chicken. Try to buy a free-range or organic chicken, as the flavor is always so much better.

Baked Indian-spiced Chicken with Cardamom and Cilantro Bulgur Wheat

1. Place all the marinade ingredients into a large non-metallic bowl and mix until well combined.

2. Slash the legs of the chicken several times with a sharp knife—this will give you lovely crispy skin once cooked. Add the chicken to the bowl and rub the marinade all over the chicken, inside and out. Cover with plastic wrap and place in the fridge for at least 4 hours (and up to 24 hours, if you have time). Alternatively, you can put the chicken and marinade into a large resealable food bag before putting it into the fridge.

3. Remove the chicken from the fridge 30 minutes before you want to put it in the oven. Preheat the oven to 450°F (400°F fan).

4. Arrange the sliced onions over the base of a large oval casserole dish, drizzle with the oil, and season with salt and pepper. Sit the chicken on top of the onions, which will act as a "trivet." Put the lemon halves inside the cavity of the chicken, cover with the lid, and place in the oven. Reduce the heat to 400°F (350°F fan) and roast for 40 minutes.

5. Remove the lid and roast for another 20 minutes, basting the chicken after 10 minutes.

6. Meanwhile, prepare the bulgur wheat. Crush the cardamom pods with the back of a knife and place them in a bowl with the bulgur wheat. Add the vegetable bouillon powder and pour in boiling water to just cover. Cover with plastic wrap and leave until all the water has been absorbed and the bulgur wheat is nice and plump, about 8 minutes. Use a fork to fluff up the bulgur wheat and then fold in the cilantro and almonds.

7. Let the chicken rest for 10 minutes before carving. Serve with the bulgur wheat.

Serves 4

1 3-lb whole chicken
2 large onions, thickly sliced
1 tbsp vegetable oil
1 lemon, halved
Sea salt and freshly ground black pepper

For the marinade

2 large garlic cloves, crushed
1 tbsp grated fresh ginger
1 tsp ground cumin
2 tsps ground coriander
2 tsps garam masala
1 tsp hot paprika
1 tbsp ground turmeric
2 tbsps vegetable oil
1 cup plain yogurt
Sea salt and freshly ground black pepper

For the bulgur wheat

3 cardamom pods
1¼ cups bulgur wheat
2 tsps vegetable bouillon powder
Handful of fresh cilantro, roughly chopped
1 cup toasted sliced almonds

Pomegranate Molasses Chicken with Roasted Vegetable Bulgur Salad

Roast chicken in any guise tends to grab my attention, and this ruby red, glistening one is rather easy to prepare. If you haven't used pomegranate molassses before, it is a worthwhile pantry ingredient. I use it mainly in beet hummus, where it adds both sweet and slightly sour notes, but it is its thick, molasses-like consistency that makes it an ideal glaze for meats, particularly chicken.

Serves 4–6

1 large free-range chicken, spatchcocked (ask your butcher to do this for you)

6 tbsps pomegranate molasses, plus extra for brushing

4 garlic cloves

1 red chili pepper, finely chopped

1¾ cups cooked bulgur wheat (see page 214)

Sea salt and freshly ground black pepper

For the roasted vegetables

2 carrots, cut into bite-size pieces

2 parsnips, cut into bite-size pieces

2 red onions, thinly sliced

3 tbsps olive oil

Sea salt and freshly ground black pepper

1. Place the chicken in a resealable bag with the pomegranate molasses, garlic, and chili pepper. Season with salt and pepper and mix the chicken in the bag so that it's completely coated. Place in the fridge to marinate for at least 2 hours, preferably overnight.

2. When you are ready to cook, preheat the oven to 400°F (350°F fan) and prepare the vegetables. Put the carrots, parsnips, and red onions into a large roasting pan and drizzle with the olive oil. Season with salt and pepper and toss to coat. Make space in the center of the pan and add the chicken, along with the marinade.

3. Roast the chicken in the oven for 50 minutes to 1 hour, or until it's cooked through and the juices run clear when a skewer is inserted into the thickest part of the thigh. The vegetables should also be tender at this stage. About 10 minutes before the end of the cooking time, brush the chicken with pomegranate molasses and return it to the oven.

4. Transfer the chicken to a cutting board and cover it with foil. Add the cooked bulgur wheat to the roasted vegetables in the pan and toss to coat in all the juices.

5. Cut the chicken into breast, thigh, leg, and wing portions, and place them on top of the bulgur wheat. Bring the roasting pan directly to the table and let your guests help themselves.

Sticky Sesame and Sriracha Chicken with Chopped Salad

The rise in popularity of sriracha sauce, a spicy hot sauce from Southeast Asia, is universal. Bottles of this tangy sweet substance are no longer just a staple of Thai street-food stalls, and can be found in supermarkets everywhere. It can be added to noodles and stir fries for a fiery kick or, as in this sticky chicken dish, to a crunchy salad.

Serves 4

1 tsp vegetable oil

4–8 skinless chicken thighs, cut into bite-size pieces

5 tbsps sriracha sauce

Thumb-size piece of fresh ginger, peeled and very finely chopped

Zest and juice of 1 lime

1 tbsp honey

2 tsps light soy sauce

1 tsp sesame oil

For the salad

½ head red cabbage, finely sliced

5 oz kale (about ⅓ bunch), leaves torn from stem and finely sliced

2 carrots, julienned

1 tsp sesame oil

1 red bell pepper, deseeded and cut into bite-size pieces

1 yellow bell pepper, deseeded and cut into bite-size pieces

1 cup frozen edamame beans, thawed

Handful of cashews, toasted

1 tbsp sesame seeds, toasted

Large handful of cilantro

1. Heat the oil in a wok or a large frying pan over medium-high heat and fry the chicken pieces until just browned on all sides. Add the sriracha sauce, ginger, lime zest, half the lime juice, honey, soy sauce, and sesame oil, and toss to coat. Cover and simmer for 8 minutes, or until the sauce has thickened slightly and the chicken is completely cooked through.

2. Meanwhile, prepare the salad. Place the red cabbage, kale, and carrots in a large mixing bowl with the remaining lime juice and sesame oil. Massage the kale until it becomes tender, and then mix in the remaining salad ingredients.

3. Serve the sriracha chicken with the salad, and garnish with the sesame seeds and cilantro.

This dish is really simple, but makes a truly delicious supper—the sweet and exotic flavor of sweet potato and fresh cilantro takes it to another level. I've used chicken breasts here, but chicken thighs are an excellent alternative.

Cajun Chicken with Sweet Potato Mash

1. Start preparing the sweet potato mash. Place the sweet potatoes in a metal steamer in a pan of simmering water and steam for 10–12 minutes or until just tender. You can add the broccolini for the last 5 minutes of cooking time. Remove the broccolini and keep warm.

2. Transfer the sweet potatoes to a mixing bowl and use a fork to roughly mash them together with the coconut oil and cilantro. Season with salt and pepper and keep warm.

3. Butterfly the chicken: place a chicken breast on a chopping board and, with your hand flat on the top of it, use a sharp knife to slice into the thickest part of the breast. Do not slice all the way through. Open out the chicken so it resembles a butterfly and repeat with the other chicken breast.

4. Lay the butterflied chicken on a plate and rub with the oil. Sprinkle the paprika, cayenne pepper, garlic powder, and thyme leaves all over, and season with salt and black pepper.

5. Place a large grill pan over high heat and cook the chicken for 3–4 minutes on each side, or until cooked all the way through. Serve the chicken with the sweet potato mash and broccolini.

Serves 2

1 bunch broccolini
2 skinless chicken breasts (about 5 oz each)
1 tsp vegetable oil
1 tbsp smoked paprika
1 tsp cayenne pepper
1 tsp garlic powder
3 thyme sprigs, leaves only
Sea salt and freshly ground black pepper

For the sweet potato mash
2–4 sweet potatoes, peeled and diced
1 tbsp coconut oil
Large handful of cilantro, roughly chopped
Sea salt and freshly ground black pepper

Warm Duck, Orange, Pomegranate, and Mint Salad

The combination of rich duck meat, a salty sharp dressing, the sweet tang and texture of pomegranate seeds, and the hit of freshness from the orange, mint, and cilantro make this dish particularly special. This is a super winter salad, wonderfully aromatic.

Serves 2

2 duck breasts (about 5 oz each)

½ tsp sea salt

1 tsp Chinese five-spice powder

1 large orange

4 scallions, finely sliced

2 large carrots, thinly sliced

½ cucumber, thinly sliced

½ Chinese cabbage, finely shredded

2 large handfuls of salad greens (baby spinach, baby kale, Little Gem)

Large handful of fresh mint leaves

Large handful of fresh cilantro leaves

1 pomegranate, halved

For the dressing

1 tbsp sunflower oil

1 tbsp dark soy sauce

1 tbsp honey

1 tbsp rice wine vinegar

1 tsp sesame oil

Small thumb-size piece of fresh ginger, peeled and grated

1. Preheat the oven to 400°F (350°F fan).

2. Place the duck breasts on a chopping board and score the skin diagonally with a sharp knife at ⅓-inch intervals. Rub the duck all over with the sea salt and five-spice powder.

3. Place an ovenproof frying pan over medium heat. Without waiting for the pan to get hot, place the duck breasts in the pan, skin side down, and cook for about 6 minutes, or until the skin is crispy. Tilt the pan away from you and remove the fat with a spoon. Turn the breasts over and then place the pan in the oven for 8 minutes. Transfer to a cutting board, cover with foil, and leave to rest.

4. In a bowl, whisk together all the ingredients for the dressing. Using a sharp knife, cut the top and bottom off the orange and carefully slice off the peel and white pith. Separate the orange segments and set them aside. Squeeze any remaining juice into the dressing.

5. Mix together the scallions, carrots, cucumber, Chinese cabbage, salad greens, and herbs, and toss with the dressing.

6. Arrange the dressed salad on a serving plate. Top with the orange segments and thin slices of duck. Hold the pomegranate cut side down and bash the skin with a wooden spoon or rolling pin to release the seeds. Sprinkle over the dish and serve.

Spiced Lamb Shoulder with Grilled Eggplant and Bulgur Tabbouleh

Lamb shoulder is an often-underrated cut of meat. Slowly cooked and subtly spiced, it's delicious served with a simple, yet flavorful, tabbouleh and smoky, grilled eggplant.

Serves 4

2 tbsps olive oil

2 tsps ground ginger

2 tsps ground cumin

2 tsps ground coriander

2 tsps ground turmeric

3 garlic cloves

Zest and juice of 2 lemons

Small bunch of cilantro, stems chopped (leaves reserved)

Pinch of salt

1 3-lb boneless lamb shoulder

Plain yogurt, to serve

For the grilled eggplant

2 eggplants, cut lengthwise into ¼-inch-thick slices

3 tbsps extra-virgin olive oil, for brushing

1 tsp chili flakes

Sea salt and freshly ground black pepper

For the tabbouleh

¾ cup bulgur wheat

1 cup boiling water

½ cucumber, peeled and diced

3 plum tomatoes, chopped

3 scallions, finely sliced

Small handful of mint leaves, chopped

Small handful of flat-leaf parsley, chopped

Squeeze of lemon juice

1. Preheat the oven to 325°F (300°F fan).

2. Place the olive oil, ground spices, garlic, zest and juice of 1 lemon, chopped cilantro stems (reserve the leaves for later) and a good pinch of salt into a food processor (or use a mortar and pestle). Process until you have a smooth paste.

3. Put the lamb shoulder onto two large pieces of foil and make lots of incisions in the meat with a sharp knife. Rub the paste all over the meat. Add a couple tablespoons of water, then seal the foil around the lamb, leaving a little pocket of air above it. Place the lamb in a shallow roasting pan and cook it in the oven for 4 hours.

4. After this time, open the foil and baste the lamb with its juices. Leaving the foil open, cook it for another hour, by which time the lamb should be meltingly tender. Turn off the oven, but leave the lamb inside to rest.

5. For the grilled eggplant, brush the slices with olive oil, sprinkle with chili flakes, and season with salt and pepper. Heat a large grill pan over high heat and then cook the eggplant slices on both sides, until they are tender and have visible grill marks all over. Remove the eggplant from the pan and keep it warm.

6. For the tabbouleh, place the bulgur wheat in a heatproof bowl and pour in the boiling water. Cover with plastic wrap and allow to soak for 10–15 minutes. Drain away any excess liquid and then fluff up the tabbouleh with a fork, before stirring in the remaining ingredients until well combined. Taste and adjust the seasoning.

7. To serve, carve the lamb into thick slices. Arrange the eggplant on a plate, top with the tabbouleh and slices of lamb, and sprinkle with the reserved cilantro leaves. Serve with yogurt.

This salad of simple cooked steak and crisp, shaved fennel is dressed with a peppery horseradish sauce. It's not only quick to make, but is layered with wonderful fresh flavors, resulting in a winning supper that takes little effort.

Rosemary Beef with Horseradish Sauce and Fennel Salad

1. Whisk together the olive oil, garlic, and rosemary, and brush over the steaks, then season with salt and pepper.

2. Place a large grill pan over medium-high heat and cook the steaks for 2–3 minutes on each side for medium rare (adjust the timing to cook them to your liking). Remove the steaks from the pan and let them rest under foil for 5 minutes before slicing into thin strips.

3. Whisk together the ingredients for the dressing in a large bowl. Add the fennel, zucchini, and red onion, and toss to coat.

4. Divide the fennel salad between two plates and top with the arugula, pine nuts, and slices of steak.

Serves 2

1 tbsp olive oil

1 garlic clove, finely chopped

1 rosemary sprig, leaves finely chopped

2 small rib-eye steaks

Sea salt and freshly ground black pepper

For the dressing

Juice of ½ lemon

1 tbsp plain yogurt

1 tbsp fresh horseradish, grated

1 tbsp extra-virgin olive oil

2 fennel bulbs, trimmed and thinly sliced

1 zucchini, sliced into thin rounds

1 small red onion, very thinly sliced

Large handful of arugula per person

⅓ cup pine nuts, toasted

Side Dishes 4 Ways

Sesame Green Beans

Serves 4

About 4 cups green beans, trimmed

3 tbsps tahini

1 tsp dark soy sauce

1 tsp rice vinegar

2 tbsps water

3 scallions, finely sliced

2 tbsps sesame seeds, toasted

1. Blanch the green beans in a pan of boiling, salted water until just tender.

2. In a large mixing bowl, whisk together the tahini, soy sauce, rice vinegar, and enough water to loosen the mix until you have a smooth dressing.

3. Transfer the warm green beans to the tahini dressing and toss until completely coated. Serve sprinkled with scallions and sesame seeds.

Caponata

Serves 4

1½ tbsps olive oil

1 large eggplant, diced into ¼-inch chunks

1 large onion, finely chopped

2 celery stalks, finely chopped

3 garlic cloves, very finely chopped

1 red bell pepper, deseeded and cut into ⅓-inch dice

1 yellow bell pepper, deseeded and cut into ⅓-inch dice

1 14-oz can plum tomatoes

1 tbsp capers

2 tbsps red wine vinegar

¼ cup pine nuts, toasted

Large handful of basil leaves

Sea salt and freshly ground black pepper

1. Heat 1 tablespoon of the olive oil in a large frying pan over medium-high heat and fry the eggplant for 10–12 minutes, or until softened. Season to taste. Remove with a slotted spoon and transfer to a plate.

2. Add a little more oil to the pan and fry the onion, celery, garlic, and pepper for about 10 minutes, or until softened. Add the tomatoes, capers, and red wine vinegar and simmer for 10 minutes, or until the vinegar has evaporated. Season with salt and pepper and stir in the pine nuts and basil leaves. Serve immediately.

During the summer when I cook for friends and family I like the idea that the table has a selection of dishes to choose from, all of which can easily sit on the plate beside grilled meat or fish. These are four great recipes that make wonderful side dishes.

Roasted Cauliflower Doorstops

Serves 4

2 heads of cauliflower
1 onion, thickly sliced, but root left intact
1 tbsp olive oil
3 thyme sprigs, leaves only
Sea salt and freshly ground black pepper

For the lemon, garlic, and thyme dressing

3 tbsps extra-virgin olive oil
1 garlic clove, finely chopped
3 thyme sprigs
Zest and juice of 1 lemon

1. Preheat the oven to 400°F (350°F fan).

2. Cut the cauliflower into thick slices, about ⅓-inch thick. You should get 3–4 decent slices per head of cauliflower, but you can roast the smaller pieces alongside. Lay the cauliflower and onion slices on a large baking tray. Rub all over with olive oil and sprinkle with thyme leaves and salt and pepper.

3. Roast the cauliflower in the oven for 40 minutes, or until it is slightly charred around the edges. Whisk together all the ingredients for the dressing.

4. Remove the cauliflower and onion slices from the oven and arrange them on a large serving platter. Drizzle with the dressing and serve immediately.

Marinated Zucchini

Serves 4

2 large zucchini, cut into 4-inch batons
Table salt
3 tbsps extra-virgin olive oil
3 tbsps white wine vinegar
1 garlic clove, very finely chopped
½ tsp red chili flakes
1 tbsp dried oregano

1. Place the zucchini in a colander and sprinkle it all over with salt. Let it sit over a sink for 1–2 hours to allow any moisture to drain away.

2. Squeeze any remaining liquid from the zucchini and then transfer it to bowl. Pour in the olive oil, white wine vinegar, chili flakes, and oregano. Toss to coat, then cover the zucchini and allow it to sit in the fridge for 1–2 hours or overnight.

3. Remove the zucchini from the fridge 30 minutes before serving, to allow it to come to room temperature.

desserts and sweet treats

There is no way, in my quest for a more balanced lifestyle and diet, that I could skimp on the sweet stuff. I always have room for dessert, even after the biggest meal. At the mere mention of cake, my eyes go wide! Dessert, I would argue, is that important shift in gear, that icing on the cake, that wonderful end to a delicious meal. While many people who are eating cleaner diets and lighter foods might steer clear of desserts, the recipes here provide some inspirational options that are light, bright, fresh, and delicious. Taking into account a range of dietary needs, this is a collection of some of my favorite desserts, many of which just happen to be gluten-free, sugar-free, or dairy-free. Most of them are jam-packed with fresh fruit and—in some cases—a few vegetables have been snuck in there, too!

The simplicity of clever cooking at home is demonstrated here, with recipes like Fragrant Roasted Rhubarb, scented with ginger and orange and served with cool yogurt and a sprinkle of vibrant green pistachios; freshly sliced Orange and Pomegranate Salad with Orange Blossom Cream; and delightfully sharp and sweet Green Apple Sorbet. Lighter baked treats are also featured, like my moist Carrot and Zucchini Cake with Rosemary and Orange Crème Fraîche; the ridiculously addictive and chewy Coconut Macaroons; or my rich, dairy-free Peanut Butter Brownies drizzled with dark chocolate.

The desserts in this chapter aren't for every day. Instead, they provide great options for lighter dinner party meals or treats for special occasions. When following a healthy diet, it's important to keep a real balance and still include food that excites you, which is where recipes like these come in. So you really *can* have your cake and eat it, too!

Fragrant Roasted Rhubarb with Pistachio Nuts

Every year in my garden one of the first plants to make an appearance is rhubarb. The vibrant pink stalks can be used in so many different desserts and even savory dishes, but my favorite way of making rhubarb shine is this simple process of slow-roasting until they are tender. The low temperature and cooking time results in rhubarb stalks that hold both their color and shape. Once cooked, they can be enjoyed with granola for breakfast, spooned hot over ice cream, or served simply like this, with yogurt, honey, and nuts.

Serves 4

1¼ lbs young rhubarb (about 6 stalks)

2 oranges

3 tbsps orange blossom honey

2 whole star anise

Small thumb-size piece of fresh ginger, peeled and thinly sliced

1 vanilla bean, split lengthwise

¼ cup shelled pistachios, roughly chopped

Plain yogurt, to serve

1. Preheat the oven to 275°F (250°F fan).

2. Trim the rhubarb and then cut across on the diagonal into 2-inch pieces. Put into a ceramic baking dish large enough to fit all the rhubarb in a single layer snugly. Use a peeler to pare thin strips of orange zest off one of the oranges and add them to the rhubarb, then squeeze the juice of both oranges. Drizzle with honey and orange juice.

3. Add the star anise, ginger, and vanilla bean, tucking them in so that they can give the maximum flavor. Cover tightly with foil and roast for 40 minutes.

4. Remove from the oven and allow to cool, leaving the foil in place for 10 minutes.

5. To serve, sprinkle the roasted rhubarb with the chopped pistachios and bring the dish straight to the table with a bowl of yogurt so everyone can help themselves.

This is a mouthwateringly good dessert that should be made when citrus fruits are in season and at their best. Feel free to use a mixture of blood oranges, clementines, and regular oranges. You can make this several hours in advance, cover with plastic wrap and chill, then just sprinkle with the pistachios before serving.

Orange and Pomegranate Salad with Orange Blossom Cream

1. To make the orange blossom cream, whisk the orange blossom water into the yogurt and then fold in the mint, if using. Transfer to a serving dish, cover with plastic wrap, and chill until needed.

2. Using a sharp knife, take a slice from the bottom and top of each orange, then place on a chopping board and carefully cut away the skin and pith, following the curve of the orange. Cut the fruit into horizontal slices, reserving any juice in a small bowl.

3. Arrange the orange slices on a large glass plate. Cut the pomegranate in half and, holding the cut side of the pomegranate over the oranges, bash with a rolling pin so that the seeds tumble out.

4. Mix the orange blossom water with the reserved orange juice, then drizzle over the top of the salad and sprinkle with the pistachios. Serve with the bowl of orange blossom cream on the side so your guests can help themselves.

Serves 4

4 oranges

1 pomegranate

2 tbsps orange blossom water

¼ cup shelled pistachios, roughly chopped

For the orange blossom cream

1 tsp orange blossom water

½ cup coconut yogurt

1 tsp shredded fresh mint (optional)

Raspberry and Lime Chia Seed Pudding

This chia seed pudding has to be the ultimate guilt-free dessert; sometimes I even have it for breakfast. I'm a big fan of chia seeds—they have no taste so they take on the flavor of whatever you mix them with. When soaked in liquid overnight, the seeds expand to more than triple their original size.

Serves 4

2 cups raspberries

½ cup low-fat coconut milk

1 cup almond milk

⅓ cup chia seeds

1 tbsp shredded coconut

2–3 tsps honey or maple syrup, to taste

Finely grated zest and juice of 1 lime

Coconut flakes, to decorate

1. Put half the raspberries in a large bowl and mash with a fork, then add all the remaining ingredients, except the whole raspberries and coconut flakes. Stir well to combine. Cover with plastic wrap and chill in the fridge for at least 6 hours, ideally overnight.

2. Divide the pudding into glass serving dishes and top with the remaining raspberries and a few coconut flakes.

Green Apple Sorbet

This green apple sorbet is a very clever way to make a sorbet without any fuss. It would also work well with frozen mango or peach chunks, mixed summer berries, or pretty much any fruit you like. Agave nectar is a natural liquid sweetener from South Africa and Mexico, where it is used to make tequila. It is actually sweeter than honey, and has a high fructose content. For a novel way to finish a meal, try pouring a little tequila into the bottom of each serving glass, then scoop the sorbet on top.

Serves 4–6

6 Granny Smith apples, quartered and cored

Juice of 1 large lemon

⅓–⅔ cups agave nectar

Fresh mint sprigs, to decorate (optional)

1. Cut the apple quarters in half crosswise and toss them in a tablespoon of the lemon juice. Arrange on a baking tray and place in the freezer for at least 2 hours, or preferably overnight, until completely hard.

2. Remove the frozen apple pieces from the freezer and allow to thaw for 10 minutes before placing in the food processor with the remaining lemon juice and 4 tablespoons of the agave nectar. Process until just combined and then pour just enough of the remaining agave nectar through the feed tube to give you a smooth purée that has the consistency of a sorbet.

3. Transfer the mixture to a plastic container with a lid and freeze for 3–4 hours, or until firm. This keeps well in the freezer for up to two weeks. Leave in the fridge for 10 minutes before scooping and arranging in small, glass serving dishes. Decorate with mint sprigs, if you like, before serving.

Glazed Apple Galettes

A good fruit galette has to be one of the most delicious things to eat. However, it is only as good as its components—choose a fairly tart eating apple, such as Granny Smith or Braeburn, and take the time to make the pastry, being careful not to overwork it. I like to serve this with Calvados crème fraîche, which is simply a container of crème fraîche with a couple of tablespoons of Calvados stirred into it.

Serves 6

3–5 eating apples, peeled, cored, and very thinly sliced

2 tbsps butter, melted

2–3 tbsps light muscovado sugar (or light brown sugar)

Confectioners' sugar, for dusting (optional)

Calvados crème fraîche, to serve (see above)

For the pastry

Scant 2 cups fine spelt flour, plus extra for dusting

1½ sticks butter, diced and well chilled

1 medium free-range egg

1 tbsp balsamic vinegar

1 tsp sea salt

2 tbsps ice-cold water

1. First make the pastry. Place the flour and butter in a bowl and, using a butter knife, cut the butter into the flour until you have a rough pebble-like mixture.

2. Whisk together the egg with the balsamic vinegar and sea salt. Add this to the butter and flour and, using two forks, gently toss through until the dough begins to come together. Add a little cold water to bring the dough to a rough ball.

3. Turn the pastry out onto parchment paper or plastic wrap, wrap tightly and chill in the fridge for at least 30 minutes (overnight is fine).

4. Preheat the oven to 450°F (400°F fan) and line 2 large baking trays with parchment paper.

5. Roll out the pastry on a lightly floured surface until it is about ⅛-inch thick, then cut it into 6 circles about 5½ inches in diameter. Arrange them on the lined baking trays. Arrange the apple slices on each pastry circle in an overlapping circle, leaving a ¾-inch pastry border that is uncovered. Brush lightly with melted butter, then lightly sprinkle with the sugar. Gently fold the pastry border over the apples.

6. Bake the tarts for 15 minutes, or until the pastry is golden and the apples are cooked through. Serve while still warm, but not burning hot, dusted with a little confectioners' sugar, if desired. Add a spoonful of the Calvados crème fraîche, and be thankful for what you have!

This is a great recipe for a dinner party, but you will need to flex your whisking muscles! It's really a fragrant orange jelly, topped with a sabayon, which, when made correctly, will be as light as a feather. It is important to whisk it continuously while it cools to keep it from splitting.

Grown-up Jelly and Custard

1. Using a sharp knife, take a slice from the bottom and top of each orange, then place on a cutting board and carefully cut away the skin and pith, following the curve of the orange. Cut the fruit into segments and arrange in the bottom of 4 martini glasses. Set aside.

2. Place the gelatine in a bowl of cold water and set aside to soften for 10 minutes. Drain and gently squeeze dry. Place in a small pan with a drop of the wine and heat gently until dissolved.

3. Warm the remaining wine in a separate pan and stir into the dissolved gelatine mixture. Pass through a fine sieve into a pitcher. Pour the mixture over the orange segments, trying not to disturb the fruit too much. Leave to cool completely and then chill for 3 hours, until softly set.

4. Once the jellies are set, make the sabayon. Place the orange juice in a small pan with the wine and bring to a boil over high heat. Reduce the heat and continue to simmer for 15–20 minutes, or until the liquid has reduced to about 3 tablespoons. It will be quite thick and syrupy.

5. Place the egg yolks in a heatproof bowl and add the reduced orange juice and wine mixture and sugar. Set over a pan of simmering water, making sure the bottom of the bowl doesn't touch the water, and whisk for 8–10 minutes, until thick and foamy. The sabayon is ready when the mixture is thick and holds its shape when you lift the whisk and let some of the mixture drop back into the bowl. Remove it from the heat and set it in a bowl of ice. Continue whisking it until the sabayon has cooled completely.

6. Remove the glasses from the fridge and spoon the cooled sabayon on top. These can be served at once or chilled for up to 24 hours. Decorate with the chopped pistachio nuts and mint leaves just before serving.

Serves 4

2 oranges

3 tsps unflavored powdered gelatin

2½ cups Sauternes or Orange Muscat

For the sabayon

½ cup freshly squeezed orange juice, sieved

1¼ cups Sauternes or Orange Muscat

3 large free-range egg yolks

2 tbsps superfine sugar

Chopped shelled pistachio nuts and mint leaves, to decorate

Chocolate Avocado Pudding

A sweet and surprisingly delicious little dessert that will guarantee to have your guests guessing what the secret ingredient is.

Serves 4

3 ripe avocados, pitted, flesh scooped out

Heaping ½ cup cocoa powder

1 tsp espresso powder

3 tbsps honey

3 tbsps coconut milk

1 tsp vanilla extract

½ tsp sea salt, plus extra for sprinkling

1 tbsp raw cacao nibs, plus extra for sprinkling

1. Place the avocados, cocoa powder, espresso powder, honey, coconut milk, vanilla extract, and sea salt in a food processor and process until smooth. Stir in the raw cacao nibs.

2. Transfer the mixture to 4 individual serving dishes, cover with plastic wrap, and chill in the fridge for 30 minutes, until slightly firm.

3. When ready to serve, sprinkle with a little more sea salt and raw cacao nibs.

This crust uses fresh dates, which are available year round but are at their best between November and January. Fresh dates should be plump and moist with glossy skins. To remove the pits, just push them out with your finger.

Dark Chocolate and Orange Tart

1. For the crust, place the almonds in a food processor and blend for 1 minute, then add the dates, coconut oil, salt, and raw cocoa powder and continue to blend until well combined.

2. Line the removable base of a 9-inch fluted tart pan with parchment paper and reassemble the pan. Transfer the crust mixture to the pan. Use your fingers to spread it evenly across the base of the pan, and press it into the fluted sides. Cover with plastic wrap and chill for at least 30 minutes while you make the filling.

3. To make the filling, clean out the bowl of the food processor and add the dates, orange zest and juice, honey, coconut oil, and raw cocoa powder. Blend together until smooth and then, using a plastic spatula, scrape the filling into the chilled crust and smooth the top with an offset spatula. Chill for at least 2 hours, ideally overnight.

4. To serve, remove the tart from the pan and lightly dust it with the cocoa powder and grated orange zest before cutting the tart into slices.

Serves 6–8

8 fresh dates, pitted
Finely grated zest and juice of 1 orange
½ cup orange blossom honey
¼ cup coconut oil, melted
1 cup raw cocoa powder

For the crust
2 cups blanched almonds
12 fresh dates, pitted
3 tbsps melted coconut oil
Pinch of sea salt
1 tbsp raw cocoa powder

To decorate
Raw cocoa powder
Finely grated zest of 1 orange

Mocha Chocolate Mousse

Everyone loves chocolate mousse, and this one has a wonderfully light and airy texture. It is quick and easy to make, and is best served the day after it's made. What's not to love?

Serves 4–6

9 oz dark chocolate (85% cacao mass)
6 medium free-range eggs, separated
4 tbsps strong black coffee
4 tbsps almond milk
Chocolate espresso beans, to decorate

1. Melt the chocolate in a large bowl set over a pan of gently simmering water, making sure the bottom of the bowl doesn't touch the water. Remove the bowl from the heat and let the melted chocolate cool down to room temperature.

2. Once the melted chocolate is at room temperature, whisk in the egg yolks one at a time, and then gently fold in the coffee and almond milk.

3. Using a hand-held electric mixer and a clean bowl, whisk the egg whites until stiff peaks form, then mix 1–2 tablespoons of the beaten egg whites into the chocolate mixture to loosen it. Gently fold in the remainder, using a large metal spoon.

4. Transfer the mousse to individual glasses and smooth the surface. Cover with plastic wrap and chill for at least 2 hours, ideally overnight. Decorate with chocolate espresso beans before serving.

Sticky Toffee Pudding with Roasted Figs

This recipe borrows all the best bits from a traditional sticky toffee pudding, but uses figs instead of dates. The result is a dense and rich warm sponge cake smothered in a slightly alternative caramel and proudly presented with soft roasted figs. Just try to resist!

Serves 8

20 ready-to-eat dried figs, chopped

1 tsp baking soda

1½ sticks butter

1 cup light muscovado sugar (or light brown sugar)

2 large free-range eggs

1⅔ cups self-rising flour

1 tsp vanilla extract

For the roasted figs

8 firm, ripe fresh figs, sliced in half

2 tbsps honey

For the date caramel

2½ oz dates, chopped

4 tbsps coconut oil, melted

1. Preheat the oven to 350°F (325°F fan) and grease and line an 8 x 8 inch baking pan with parchment paper.

2. To roast the fresh figs, arrange the figs in a ceramic baking dish, cut side up, and drizzle with the honey. Roast for about 15 minutes until the figs are cooked through but still hold their shape. Remove from the oven and cool at room temperature.

3. Put the dried figs and 1¼ cups water in a pan and place over medium-high heat. Bring the mixture to a boil and then simmer for approximately 20 minutes, or until the liquid has reduced by half and the figs have softened. Use a hand-held stick blender to purée the mixture until smooth, then stir in the baking soda. Set aside.

4. Using a hand-held mixer, cream the butter and sugar in a large bowl until light and pale. Add one egg at a time, mixing after each addition, until they are incorporated—if you add the eggs all at once, the mixture can split.

5. Fold the puréed figs, flour, and vanilla extract into the pudding mixture until you have a smooth batter. Pour it into the prepared baking pan and bake for 20–25 minutes.

6. Meanwhile, prepare the date caramel. Put the chopped dates into a pan with ¾ cup water and cook gently until softened, about 5 minutes. Transfer to a food processor, add the melted coconut oil, and process until smooth.

7. Check the cake—it should have risen and be firm to the touch, and a toothpick inserted into the center should come out clean. Remove the cake from the oven and allow it to cool slightly before slicing into 8 generous portions.

8. To serve, spoon some date caramel sauce over each pudding, and top with a couple of roasted fig halves.

Lemon and Blueberry Cheesecake

This cheesecake is extra easy because it does not require any gelatin; the action of the lemon juice on the mascarpone and crème fraîche helps it set all on its own. The crust uses gingersnaps, which can be found just about everywhere.

Serves 8

Finely grated zest and juice of 4 lemons
14 tbsps honey
1¼ lbs mascarpone cream
1¾ cups crème fraîche
2 cups blueberries

For the crust

3½ oz Brazil nuts
3½ oz gingersnaps, roughly broken up
18 medjool dates, pitted and chopped
3 tbsps coconut oil, melted
Pinch of sea salt

1. Line an 8-inch springform cake pan with parchment paper.

2. For the crust, put the Brazil nuts into a food processor with the gingersnaps and process until you have fine crumbs. Add the dates, coconut oil, and salt and blend again until the mixture is just beginning to stick together. Transfer the mixture to the prepared cake pan and press it down firmly to create a thin, even layer. Chill in the fridge for 30 minutes while you make the filling.

3. For the filling, put the lemon zest and juice and the honey into a food processor and blend until well combined. Put the mascarpone and crème fraîche into a large bowl and gently fold in the honey and lemon mixture until evenly combined and smooth. Use an offset spatula to spread the mixture over the crust, then chill in the fridge for at least 4 hours to firm up, ideally overnight.

4. Remove the cheesecake from the pan and transfer to a serving plate. Pile the blueberries on top to serve.

This pudding recipe is based on an absolute classic—the definitive yogurt cake from a fantastic restaurant in London called Moro. It's delicious served warm or chilled. Orange blossom water is now readily available at most large supermarkets or from specialty food stores. It has a beautifully fragrant flavor and is a welcome addition to all sorts of drinks and sorbets. Serve it with thick Greek yogurt, with a splash of vanilla extract, or stir the seeds from a vanilla bean through the yogurt.

Orange Blossom, Yogurt, and Pistachio Pudding

1. Preheat the oven to 325°F (300°F fan) and line a 9-inch springform cake pan with parchment paper.

2. Place the egg yolks in a large bowl with about three-quarters of the sugar and beat until light in color, using a hand-held electric mixer or wooden spoon. Beat in the vanilla seeds, then fold in the spelt flour, orange blossom water, and lemon zest and juice until well combined. Finally stir in the yogurt, almond milk, and half the pistachio nuts.

3. Whisk the egg whites in a separate large bowl with the remaining sugar until stiff peaks form, using either a hand-held electric mixer (make sure you clean the beaters) or a balloon whisk. Stir one spoonful of the beaten egg whites into the yogurt mixture to loosen it, then fold in the remaining egg whites, being careful not to knock out too much air.

4. Spoon the mixture into the prepared cake pan and then place it in a roasting pan half-filled with boiling water. Bake on the middle rack of the oven for 20 minutes. Remove from the oven and sprinkle with the remaining pistachio nuts, then increase the heat to 350°F (325°F fan) and return the cake to the oven for another 20 minutes, until it has risen and is golden brown. Remove the cake from the oven and let it cool for about 5 minutes. Don't worry if it drops slightly—that's supposed to happen.

5. Spoon the pudding onto warmed plates; the base should be like a wet custard with a light sponge on top. Add a dollop of vanilla-spiked Greek yogurt to each one to serve.

Serves 4

3 large free-range eggs, separated

6 tbsps superfine sugar

2 vanilla beans, split lengthwise and seeds scraped out

1 tbsp fine spelt flour

2 tbsps orange blossom water

Finely grated zest and juice of 1 lemon

1 cup thick Greek yogurt

2 tbsps almond milk

¼ cup shelled pistachio nuts, roughly chopped

Vanilla-spiked Greek yogurt, to serve (see above)

Coconut Cake with Passion Fruit and Mango

All the flavors used for this cake come together brilliantly to create a crave-worthy dessert or snack. It looks absolutely stunning and will have your friends begging for the recipe. . . . You have been warned!

Serves 4–6

For the coconut cake

3 large eggs

¾ cup superfine sugar

¾ cup sunflower seed spread, at room temperature, plus extra for greasing

1 cup dried, unsweetened coconut

Juice of 1 orange

⅓ cup gluten-free flour, plus extra for dusting

1 tbsp gluten-free baking powder

For the passion fruit frosting

¾ cup sunflower seed spread

2 cups confectioners' sugar, sifted

Generous pinch of sea salt flakes

½ tsp vanilla extract

2–3 passion fruits, halved, pulp scooped out and sieved to remove the seeds

To decorate

1 large firm ripe mango, peeled and cut into thin slices

1 passion fruit, halved

1 heaping tbsp lightly toasted coconut flakes (optional)

1. Preheat the oven to 350°F (325°F fan). Lightly grease an 8-inch-square nonstick baking pan and then lightly dust with flour or line with parchment paper.

2. Using a hand-held electric mixer, beat the eggs and sugar together in a large bowl until light and fluffy. Add the sunflower seed spread, coconut, and orange juice and beat again until well mixed.

3. Sift the flour and baking powder into another bowl and then fold into the egg mixture, using a large metal spoon. Transfer to the prepared baking pan and bake for about 20 minutes, or until well-risen and golden brown and a toothpick inserted into the center comes out clean. Let cool in the pan for 5 minutes, then transfer to a wire rack to cool completely.

4. Meanwhile make the passion fruit frosting. Place the sunflower seed spread in a free-standing mixer. Add half the confectioners' sugar and mix for 1–2 minutes to combine. Switch off the machine, scrape down the sides of the bowl with a spatula, and add the salt and vanilla extract. Switch back on again, add the rest of the confectioners' sugar, and mix until combined. Drizzle in enough of the sieved passion fruit purée to make a nice smooth frosting, scraping down the sides again with the spatula if necessary. Cover with plastic wrap and chill.

5. To serve, spread the passion fruit frosting over the cake with a spatula and then arrange the mango slices on top. Spoon the passion fruit pulp on top and sprinkle with the lightly toasted coconut flakes, if using.

Fig, Honey, and Almond Cake

Gently spiced and with added texture from the sliced almonds, this cake comes together with a drizzle of sweet, floral honey. Do use muscovado sugar if you can, as it is relatively unrefined with much or all of the molasses still remaining, which gives it a slightly fudgy, more caramelized flavor. Some cheaper brown sugars are just refined sugar that has been colored, with none of the authentic flavor.

Serves 6–8

1 stick butter, plus extra for greasing

1 cup light muscovado sugar (or light brown sugar)

2 large free-range eggs

Heaping ½ cup all-purpose flour, sifted

1 tsp baking powder

Pinch of salt

1 tsp ground cinnamon

2 tsps ground cardamom

12 firm, ripe fresh figs, sliced in half

½ cup sliced almonds

Floral honey, to drizzle

Vanilla yogurt, to serve

1. Preheat the oven to 350°F (325°F fan) and grease and line an 8-inch springform cake pan with parchment paper.

2. Using a hand-held electric mixer, beat the butter and sugar in a large bowl until pale. Add the eggs, one at a time, mixing until they are incorporated. Fold in the flour, baking powder, salt, cinnamon, and cardamom until you have a thick cake batter.

3. Finely chop 6 of the figs, leaving the rest cut in halves. Stir in the chopped figs and pour the batter into the prepared cake pan. The batter will be thick, so use a spatula to spread it across the base of the pan. Gently press the fig halves, cut side up, into the batter and sprinkle the almonds on top.

4. Bake for 40–45 minutes, or until a toothpick inserted into the center comes out clean. Check after 30 minutes and cover the cake with foil if the almonds are browning too much.

5. Remove the cake from the oven and let it cool in the pan. While the cake is still warm, prick it all over with a skewer and drizzle it with honey, letting it seep into the holes. Serve generous slices of the cake, with a dollop of the vanilla yogurt.

Carrot, zucchini, and cardamom create a wonderful combination of flavors. The cake itself is moist enough to serve on its own, but for that extra special touch, fill and top it with this delicious rosemary and orange crème fraîche. The cake will keep in the fridge for 3–5 days.

Carrot and Zucchini Cake with Rosemary and Orange Crème Fraîche

1. Preheat the oven to 350°F (325°F fan). Lightly oil two 9-inch springform cake pans and line the bases with parchment paper.

2. Prepare the rosemary and orange crème fraîche. Pour the orange juice through a sieve into a small pan with the rosemary sprigs and half the sugar, and simmer until reduced by half. Remove from the heat and allow to cool completely, then remove the rosemary sprigs and discard. Fold into the crème fraîche, then cover and chill.

3. In a large bowl, mix together the flour, baking soda, cinnamon, and cardamom. In a free-standing mixer (or in a large bowl, using a hand-held electric mixer), whisk together the sugar and eggs until pale and fluffy. With the mixer still on, pour the oil into the bowl in a steady stream and mix until it is completely incorporated, then mix in the vanilla extract.

4. Sift the dry ingredients into the batter and fold in with a spatula until just combined. Add the finely grated carrot and zucchini and fold in until completely incorporated. Divide the batter between the two lined cake pans and bake for 30 minutes, or until a toothpick inserted into the center comes out clean.

5. Remove the cakes from the oven and set them aside to cool on a wire rack. When the pans are cool enough to touch, gently release the cakes and return them to the rack, removing the parchment paper. Allow them to cool completely.

6. If one of the cakes has risen more than the other, simply trim the excess with a bread knife so that you have a flat surface to work with. Assemble the cake by spreading one of the layers with half the rosemary and orange crème fraîche. Place the second layer on top and spread with the remaining crème fraîche. Decorate with the carrot shavings and rosemary sprigs.

Serves 8

2¼ cups self-rising flour

½ tsp baking soda

1 tsp ground cinnamon

1 tsp cardamom pods, lightly crushed and seeds ground

1 cup superfine sugar

4 large free-range eggs

1 cup vegetable oil, plus extra for greasing

1 tbsp vanilla extract

2 cups carrots, finely grated

7 oz zucchini (1 small), trimmed and finely grated (squeeze out any excess moisture)

For the rosemary and orange crème fraîche

Juice of 2 oranges

2 small fresh rosemary sprigs

2 tbsps superfine sugar

1¾ cups crème fraîche

To decorate

Carrot shavings

Rosemary sprigs

Gluten-free Chocolate Celebration Cake

This cake is good enough to serve on any number of occasions and keeps well in the fridge for several days, as the liquid from the ricotta seeps into the sponge and keeps it lovely and moist. You can make this cake in advance—when it has cooked and cooled, cover it competely in plastic wrap and place it in the fridge. Then, when you're ready to serve the cake, allow it to come to room temperature before splitting and filling it.

Serves 8

4 large free-range eggs, separated

1 cup superfine sugar

4 tbsps good-quality cocoa powder, sifted

3 cups ground almonds

1 tsp baking soda, sifted

7 tbsps almond milk

For the filling

1¼ lbs ricotta cheese

4 tbsps thick honey

2 oz dark chocolate, finely grated (70% cacao mass)

1. Preheat the oven to 350°F (325°F fan) and line a 9-inch springform pan with parchment paper.

2. Place the egg yolks and sugar in a large bowl and, using a hand-held electric mixer, beat until pale and fluffy. Fold in the cocoa, almonds, and baking soda. Loosen with the milk until you have a smooth batter.

3. Using a hand-held electric mixer, beat the egg whites until stiff peaks form. Fold the egg whites into the batter, a third at a time, being careful not to knock out too much air. Transfer the batter to the prepared cake pan and smooth down the surface with an offset spatula.

4. Bake the cake for about 25–30 minutes, or until the sponge has begun to shrink away from the sides, and a toothpick inserted into the center comes out clean. Remove from the oven and run a knife around the edge of the cake. Let cool completely in the pan.

5. For the filling, place the ricotta and honey in a food processor and blend until smooth. Fold in half of the grated chocolate.

6. Remove the cake from the pan and peel off the parchment paper. Use a serrated bread knife to carefully cut it in half horizontally. Spread half of the ricotta and honey mixture over one half, and sandwich back together with the other half. Carefully spread the rest of the ricotta and honey mixture on top and sprinkle the remaining grated chocolate on top. Set the cake aside in a cool place until needed.

Fudgy Chocolate Bounty Cake

A deep, dark chocolate cake is the perfect dessert to celebrate with. This one is unique in that it doesn't require flour to bind it, but instead relies on ground almonds and dried coconut, making it gluten-free but also resulting in a rich and moist finish. With a glossy chocolate glaze and a topping of toasted coconut, this cake will be a true showstopper, whatever the occasion!

Serves 8

8 oz dark chocolate, finely chopped
 (70% cacao mass)

1 stick butter, diced

Scant 1 cup superfine sugar

1 tsp vanilla extract

1 cup ground almonds

½ cup diced coconut, plus 4 tbsp
 to decorate

6 large free-range eggs, separated

For the chocolate glaze

4 oz dark chocolate, broken into squares
 (70% cacao mass)

2 tbsps butter

⅓ cup confectioners' sugar, sifted

4 tbsps cream

1. Preheat the oven to 350° F (325°F fan) and line an 8-inch springform pan with parchment paper.

2. For the cake, melt the chocolate and butter in a large heatproof bowl set over a pan of barely simmering water. Remove the bowl from the heat and mix in the sugar, vanilla extract, ground almonds, and coconut with a spatula. Stir in the egg yolks, one at a time, mixing after each addition, until you have a thick batter.

3. Put the egg whites in a stand mixer (or use a hand-held electric mixer) and whisk until stiff peaks form. Add the egg whites to the chocolate batter, a third at a time, and fold in gently until just combined.

4. Pour the chocolate batter into the prepared cake pan and bake for about 35 minutes, until it is firm but with a slight wobble. Remove the cake from the oven and set it on a wire rack to cool in the pan. Let cool completely before removing from the pan.

5. Melt the chocolate and butter for the chocolate glaze, as above. As soon as it is melted, remove it from the heat and whisk in the confectioners' sugar and cream. Allow to cool until the mixture becomes thick enough for the whisk to leave a figure eight on the surface. Pour the glaze over the chocolate cake and then sprinkle it with the coconut. Let the cake set before slicing and serving it.

These dairy- and gluten-free muffins are the perfect start to the day with a strong cup of tea. All children love muffins and enjoy helping when it comes to baking and eating them. Replace the raspberries with blueberries, or even dried cranberries, for a different result.

Raspberry and Almond Muffins

1. Preheat the oven to 350°F (325°F fan) and line a 12-hole muffin pan with cupcake liners.

2. Beat the sunflower seed spread and sugar together in a large bowl until pale and fluffy. Add the eggs one at a time, whisking after each addition until completely combined. Stir in the vanilla extract.

3. Sift in the flour, baking powder, and baking soda, and then fold in, but don't mix much at this stage. Fold in the ground almonds and almond milk. Finally, gently fold in the raspberries until they're evenly dispersed.

4. Divide the muffin mixture among the cupcake liners, filling each two-thirds full. Bake for 20 minutes, or until golden brown and a toothpick inserted in the center comes out clean.

5. Let the muffins cool slightly in the pan before turning them out onto a wire rack to cool completely. Serve topped with raspberries. These are best eaten on the day they are made.

Makes 12

1 cup sunflower seed spread, at room temperature

⅔ cup superfine sugar

2 large free-range eggs

1 tsp vanilla extract

1 cup gluten-free flour

1 tsp gluten-free baking powder

½ tsp baking soda

½ cup ground almonds

7 tbsps almond milk

2 cups raspberries, plus extra for decoration

Coconut Macaroons

Crunchy on the outside and chewy in the middle, a good coconut macaroon is an irresistible thing. They are also suitable for freezing. To dress them up, dip or drizzle the baked macaroons with melted dark chocolate.

Makes 16

2 medium free-range egg whites

¾ cup sugar, sifted

¾ cup ground almonds

Few drops of almond extract

1 cup dried, unsweetened coconut

2 tbsps sweetened shredded coconut

2 oz good-quality dark chocolate, melted

1. Preheat the oven to 300°F (275°F fan). Line 2 baking trays with parchment paper.

2. Using a hand-held electric mixer, whisk the egg whites in a bowl until stiff peaks form. Lightly fold in the sugar. Gently stir in the ground almonds, almond extract, and dried coconut until the mixture forms a sticky dough.

3. Spoon heaping tablespoons of the mixture onto the lined baking trays, and shape into round mounds. Sprinkle a little shredded coconut on top of each one.

4. Bake for 25 minutes: the outer crust should be light golden, but the inside should be nice and soft. Let the macaroons cool on the baking trays for 1 minute, and then transfer them to a wire rack to cool completely. Drizzle the macaroons with dark chocolate and allow them to set before eating.

Red Velvet Beet Chocolate Cupcakes

Don't be alarmed that there are beets in these cupcakes; they help create a rich, chocolate batter with just a faint, sweet earthiness. To make a good chocolate frosting, it is really important to beat the butter properly—you'll find that it will go farther and taste lighter and fluffier that way!

Makes 12

4 oz dark chocolate, broken into squares (70% cacao mass)

7 oz cooked beets

Heaping ½ cup superfine sugar

1 stick butter, diced, at room temperature

2 large free-range eggs

6 oz self-rising flour

1 tsp baking powder

3 tbsps milk

For the chocolate frosting

7 tbsps butter, diced and chilled

1 cup confectioners' sugar, sifted

1 tsp vanilla extract

2 tbsps boiling water

6 tbsps good-quality cocoa powder

1. Preheat the oven to 350°F (325°F fan) and line a 12-hole muffin pan with cupcake liners.

2. Make the chocolate frosting first: beat the butter in a large bowl until pale and softened, using a hand-held electric mixer. Add the sugar, vanilla extract, and boiling water and whisk again until you have a thick paste. Beat for another minute until the mixture has doubled in volume. Add the cocoa powder, a tablespoon at a time. When it has all been incorporated, beat thoroughly for another minute. Cover with plastic wrap and chill.

3. For the cupcakes, melt the chocolate in a bowl over a pan of gently simmering water, making sure the bottom of the pan doesn't touch the water. Purée the cooked beets until smooth using a hand-held stick blender and then add it to the melted chocolate. Remove from heat.

4. Beat the sugar and butter together in a large bowl until light and fluffy, using a hand-held electric mixer. Whisk in the eggs, one at a time, until incorporated. Mix in the flour, baking powder, and milk and finally fold in the chocolate and beet mixture.

5. Spoon the mixture into the cupcake liners, filling each one about two-thirds full, and bake for 15–20 minutes, or until well risen and firm, and a toothpick inserted into the center comes out clean. Allow the cupcakes to stand for a minute before transferring them to a wire rack to cool.

6. Once the cupcakes are completely cool, spread the frosting on them using a small spatula.

The trick to fluffy cupcakes is to fold the wet and dry ingredients together as briefly as possible—until just combined—without worrying if the mixture still looks a little lumpy. These are best eaten on the day they are made.

Dairy-free Banana and Chocolate Chip Cupcakes with Meringue Frosting

1. Preheat the oven to 400°F (375°F fan) and line a 12-hole muffin pan with cupcake liners.

2. Mash the bananas in a bowl until smooth, then mix in the vanilla extract. Pour the oil into a bowl and beat in the eggs. Sift the flour, baking soda, and baking powder into a large bowl and stir in the sugar.

3. Pour the oil and egg mixture into the dry ingredients, followed by the mashed bananas, and stir until only just mixed. Fold in the chocolate chips and spoon into the cupcake liners, filling each two-thirds full. Bake for 20 minutes until well risen and golden, and a toothpick inserted into the center comes out clean.

4. Remove the cupcakes from the oven and allow them to cool for a minute in the pan and then transfer them to a wire rack to cool completely.

5. Meanwhile, make the meringue frosting. In the metal bowl of an electric mixer, whisk the sugar, egg whites, 2 tablespoons of cold water, lemon juice, and vanilla extract until well combined. In a large saucepan, heat 2½ cups of water until simmering. Set the mixing bowl on the rim of the saucepan so it rests there without touching the bottom of the saucepan. With a balloon whisk, continue to whisk the frosting, being careful not to let the frosting boil. Whisk until all the sugar is dissolved (otherwise you'll end up with grainy frosting). On a sugar thermometer, it should read 155–165°F.

6. Remove from the pan and return the bowl to the mixer and whisk the frosting until it is nice and glossy and stiff peaks have formed. This will take about 15–20 minutes. Spread or pipe the frosting onto the cooled cupcakes and sprinkle with grated chocolate.

Makes 12

3 very ripe bananas
1 tsp vanilla extract
½ cup vegetable oil
2 large free-range eggs
2 cups all-purpose flour
½ tsp baking soda
1 tsp baking powder
½ cup superfine sugar
¾ cup dark chocolate chips

For the meringue frosting
¾ cup sugar
3 large free-range egg whites
2 tbsps cold water
1 tsp lemon juice
1½ tsps vanilla extract
Grated chocolate, to decorate

Susan Jane's Raw Cacao Nib Fudge

When I first tasted this recipe, from my good pal Susan Jane White, I was blown away by the flavor—I couldn't believe there was no sugar in it. It really opened my mind to the possibilities of developing dessert recipes that are better for you. Be sure to give it a try and indulge in a true taste sensation.

Makes 25–30 squares

½ cup date syrup (or honey or maple syrup), plus a little extra, if necessary

3 tbsps extra-virgin coconut oil

1 12-oz jar light tahini

Pinch of sea salt flakes

2 tbsps carob powder

2 tsps vanilla extract, plus a little extra, if necessary

3 tbsps raw cacao nibs

1. Line a small container, approximately 3 x 3 inches, with plastic wrap so that it comes over the sides.

2. Melt the date syrup (or the honey or maple syrup) and coconut oil together in a pan over low heat. Add all the remaining ingredients, mashing them together with a fork and making sure the oil is well mixed in. Taste and adjust with a little more vanilla extract or syrup. Work quickly, as the oil will begin to separate from the other ingredients as soon as it starts cooling. (It needs a warm environment.)

3. Pour your gorgeous, gooey fudge into the lined container. Transfer it to the freezer for 4 hours before turning it out and cutting it into squares. Store any leftover fudge in the freezer, as it will melt quite quickly at room temperature.

There are certain tastes that instantly transport me back to being a kid. My aunt Erica used to bring us trays of these when she looked after us, and I've loved them ever since. Here I've added dried, unsweetened coconut and sunflower seeds to make them even better for you. This is a great recipe that uses ingredients you are bound to have on hand. If you want to make these dairy-free, simply replace the butter with dairy-free sunflower seed spread or extra-virgin coconut oil. These will store well for up to 1 week in an airtight container.

Oat and Seed Flapjacks

1. Preheat the oven to 350°F (325°F fan). Grease a shallow 7-inch-square baking pan and line it with parchment paper.

2. Put the rolled oats in a large bowl with the coconut and sunflower seeds.

3. Melt the butter, sugar, and maple syrup in a pan over low heat until the sugar has dissolved, then pour it into the rolled oat mixture. Mix well, then pour the mixture into the prepared pan and press down well.

4. Bake the mixture in the oven for about 20 minutes, or until it's golden brown. Allow it to cool slightly in the pan, then score lightly into finger shapes with a sharp knife and loosen around the edges.

5. When firm, remove from the pan and cool on a wire rack. Break into chunks before serving.

Makes 8–10

1 heaping cup rolled oats

¼ cup dried, unsweetened coconut

3 tbsps sunflower seeds

5 tbsps butter, plus extra for greasing

⅓ cup light muscovado sugar (or light brown sugar)

3 tbsps maple syrup

Peanut Butter Brownies with Chocolate Drizzle

This recipe combines two of my favorite things—peanut butter and brownies: together they make the most irresistible treat. Just be careful not to overcook them—the brownie should have a crust, while the middle should still be slightly moist. You'll be welcome at anyone's house with these!

Makes 24

1 cup crunchy peanut butter

8 oz dark chocolate, broken into squares (70% cacao mass)

1 cup light muscovado sugar (or light brown sugar)

3 large free-range eggs, beaten

1 tsp vanilla extract

4 tbsps almond milk

Scant 1 cup all-purpose flour

1 tsp baking powder

For the chocolate drizzle

4 oz dark chocolate, broken into squares

1. Preheat oven to 350°F (325°F fan) and line an 8 x 7-inch baking pan with parchment paper.

2. Place the peanut butter and chocolate in a heatproof bowl set over a pan of barely simmering water, making sure the bottom of the pan doesn't touch the water. Stir constantly until melted and smooth. Remove from heat.

3. With a hand-held electric mixer, whisk the sugar and eggs together for 2–3 minutes, until pale and fluffy. Slowly add the melted chocolate and peanut butter, then add the vanilla extract and almond milk and continue to whisk until thickened.

4. Sift the flour and baking powder into a separate bowl and then gently fold into the egg mixture. Using a spatula, pour the mixture into the prepared pan and bake on the middle rack of the oven for 15–20 minutes, or until the top is firm and the edge comes away slightly from the sides of the pan.

5. Once the brownies are done, remove the pan from the oven and allow it to cool slightly before transferring it to a wire rack to cool completely. While it is cooling, melt the chocolate for the drizzle in a heatproof bowl set over a pan of simmering water. Drizzle the melted chocolate over the top and allow it to set before slicing into individual brownies.

pantry

It's time to talk flavor makers! When you serve up delicious food, these extra touches and elements are what really set great home cooking apart from the humdrum. Deep and heady spice mixtures can be sprinkled over eggs, salads, or grilled meat and fish; nutritious bread and tasty crispbread can be part of the mix; simple sauces can be dolloped over cooked meat and fish; and crunchy caramelized vegetables and beans can be added to all sorts of dishes. Have I gotten your attention yet? These elements add an extra "wow" factor to any meal.

In addition, Roasted Spiced Chickpeas are the ultimate crunch factor to add to salads; Super Seed Bread toasted until it is crisp, and homemade Caraway Crispbread make perfect vessels for hummus or guacamole, while Middle Eastern spice mixes like Za'atar and Pistachio Dukkah add a real depth of flavor to any dish. In this chapter, you'll also find recipes for delicious dressings and spiced yogurts, perfect for adding a bit of zing to salads. Fill your kitchen with these little secret weapons and your whole body will thank you for it!

Pistachio Dukkah

Sprinkled on salads or served with bread and olive oil, this delicious mix of seeds and salt is a taste of North Africa and the Middle East.

Makes 1 small jar

3 tbsps coriander seeds

1 tbsp cumin seeds

1 tbsp fennel seeds

½ cup pistachio nuts, shelled

⅓ cup sesame seeds

1 tbsp sea salt

1. Toast the coriander, cumin, and fennel seeds in a dry frying pan over medium-high heat, until the seeds become aromatic.

2. Use a mortar and pestle to grind the seeds to a rough powder and set it aside.

3. Toast the pistachios and sesame seeds in a dry frying pan until they are golden, and then roughly chop them and add to the spice mix with the sea salt.

4. Transfer the mixture to an airtight container and store it for up to a month. Enjoy dukkah sprinkled over eggs, in salads, with roasted vegetables, or simply as a dip with bread and good-quality extra-virgin olive oil.

Za'atar

This spice blend from Arabic cuisine is highly addictive. I sprinkle it over grilled meat and fish or freshly baked flatbread brushed with olive oil.

Makes 1 small jar

2 tbsps sesame seeds

4 tsps cumin seeds

4 tsps ground sumac

1 tsp sea salt

Small handful of oregano leaves, chopped

1. Toast the sesame and cumin seeds in a dry frying pan over medium-high heat for about 2 minutes, until the sesame seeds are golden.

2. Place the toasted seeds in a mortar along with the sumac, sea salt, and oregano, and pound with a pestle until you have a fine, fragrant, and slightly moist powder.

3. Store in an airtight container for up to a month.

Wild Garlic Pesto

Use this simple pesto in sandwiches and grain salads, as well as stirred through pasta. You can also make it with basil, arugula, or wild nettles and a clove of garlic instead of the wild garlic leaves.

Makes about 2 cups

7 oz wild garlic leaves, stems cut off, washed and dried

¾ cup pine nuts

1¼ cups Parmesan, grated

1½ cups extra-virgin olive oil

Sea salt and freshly ground black pepper

1. Place the wild garlic, pine nuts, and Parmesan into a food processor and pulse until roughly chopped.

2. With the motor running, add the oil gradually, stopping to scrape down the sides of the bowl if necessary. Keep adding the oil until you have the right consistency. (You may need to add more if you prefer a looser pesto.) Season with salt and pepper to taste.

3. Transfer to clean jars and top with an extra drizzle of oil to create a seal. The pesto will keep in airtight jars in the fridge for at least a week.

Kale is an incredible superfood packed with vitamins and minerals. That aside, it can be transformed into one of the most addictive snacks I know—spicy kale chips! They are very easy to prepare; if you prefer them less spicy, simply replace the spice mixture with a generous sprinkle of sea salt.

Spicy Kale Chips

1. Preheat the oven to 400°F (350°F fan).

2. Wash the kale and dry it thoroughly, using a salad spinner, if you have one. Tear the leaves from the stems and then place the leaves on a large baking tray.

3. Mix the oil, spices, and salt together until they're evenly combined and then drizzle over the leaves. Massage the mixture into the kale until the leaves are completely coated.

4. Place the baking tray in the oven and cook the kale for 15–20 minutes, until the leaves are crisp. Serve immediately.

Serves 2

Half bunch curly kale
1 tbsp olive oil
1 tsp smoked paprika
1 tsp garlic powder
1 tsp cayenne pepper
Small pinch of sea salt

Salad Dressings 4 Ways

Piri Piri

Makes 1 small jar

2 red chilies, chopped

1 roasted red pepper (from a jar), chopped

1 garlic clove

Juice of 1 lemon

6 tbsps extra-virgin olive oil

Sea salt

1. Blend all the ingredients in a food processor until you have a smooth, loose consistency. If you find it too thick, you can add more olive oil or loosen it with some water.

2. Store in the fridge for up to 3–5 days.

Soy Ginger

Makes 1 small jar

2 tbsps sunflower oil

1 tbsp dark soy sauce

2 tsps rice wine vinegar

1 tsp sesame oil

Small thumb-size piece of fresh ginger, peeled and finely grated

1 garlic clove, finely grated

1 tsp sesame seeds, toasted

1. Place all the ingredients in a jar with a tight-fitting lid and shake to combine.

2. Store in the fridge for up to 3–5 days.

Whatever meal you bring to the table, a bowl of salad, served with or after it, is a great way to get extra greens into your diet. These are four of the salad dressings I come back to again and again.

French Mustard

Makes 1 small jar

3 tbsps extra-virgin olive oil

1 tbsp white wine vinegar

1 tsp Dijon mustard

1 garlic clove, finely grated

1 tsp honey

Sea salt and freshly ground black pepper

1. Whisk together the oil, vinegar, mustard, garlic, and honey in a bowl. Season to taste with salt and pepper.

2. Store in the fridge for up to 3–5 days.

Thai Herb

Makes 1 small jar

1 tbsp superfine sugar

Juice of 1 lime

3 tbsps fish sauce (*nam pla*)

1 garlic clove, finely grated

1 green chili, finely chopped

Large handful of cilantro leaves, finely chopped

1. Whisk together the sugar and lime juice in a bowl until the sugar has dissolved. Whisk in the remaining ingredients and then taste to make sure you have the perfect balance of salty, sweet, and sour. This dressing can be loosened with a tablespoon of water, if needed.

2. Store in the fridge for up to 3–5 days.

Super Seed Bread

Eating more healthily often means cutting out creature comforts like white bread, but I still crave things like toast piled with scrambled eggs or a quick snack of bread with nut butter. This bread is the real deal—thinly sliced and toasted it's the perfect vehicle for almost any topping.

Makes 1 loaf

½ cup pumpkin seeds

½ cup sunflower seeds

⅓ cup sesame seeds

9 oz rye flour

1 heaping cup whole wheat flour

2½ tsps quick-rising active dry yeast

1½ cups warm water

2 tbsps honey

1 tsp sea salt

2 tbsps extra-virgin olive oil

1. Toast the seeds in a large, dry frying pan over medium-high heat, until golden brown. Allow the seeds to cool and then transfer them to a large mixing bowl.

2. Add both flours and the yeast, and stir with a wooden spoon to combine. Make a well in the center of the bowl.

3. Measure the warm water into a mixing bowl, and then whisk in the honey, salt, and olive oil until dissolved. Pour this into the well of dry ingredients and mix them together until you are left with a firm dough. Turn the dough out onto a clean surface and roughly knead it for a minute or so. Transfer the dough back to the bowl. Cover it with plastic wrap and let it rise for 1 hour, although the dough won't change dramatically in size in that time.

4. Meanwhile preheat the oven to 400°F (350°F fan) and line a 2-lb loaf pan with parchment paper.

5. Turn the dough out and shape it into a loaf. Place it in the lined pan and bake the bread for 40 minutes, or until it is light brown. Remove the bread from the oven and allow it to cool completely in the pan on a wire rack.

Caraway Crispbread

Living with a Swede means our kitchen is never without crispbread, a staple ingredient in most Swedish homes. I've taken to making it myself, to save the suitcases filled with crumbled crispbread dreams. Thankfully, it's quite easy to make, and will keep for months stored in an airtight container. The Swedes use a *kruskavel* (a rolling pin with large studs) to roll out their crispbread, resulting in small dimples all across the surface, but it can also made flat.

Makes about 36 crispbreads

3½ cups coarse rye flour, plus extra for dusting

3 cups whole grain flour

2 tbsps caraway seeds

2½ tsps quick-rising active dry yeast

2 cups warm water

1 tsp honey

Pinch of fine sea salt

1. Combine the flours, seeds, and yeast in a mixing bowl and make a well in the center with a wooden spoon.

2. Measure the warm water into a mixing bowl and stir in the honey and salt. Pour this mixture into the well in the dry ingredients and, using a wooden spoon, slowly mix until you have a rough dough.

3. Turn the dough out onto a floured surface and knead gently for 3–4 minutes, until it becomes smooth. Form the dough into a smooth ball, return it to the bowl, and cover it with plastic wrap and a damp cloth. Leave the dough in a warm place to rise for about 1 hour, until the dough has risen slightly.

4. Preheat the oven to 425°F (400°F fan). Turn the dough out onto a floured surface and roll it into a long thin sausage, and then cut out small Ping-Pong size balls. Roll each ball out into long shapes, about ¹⁄₁₆-inch thick, and then transfer them to lightly floured baking trays. If you want to create a dimpled surface (see above), you can prick the surface with a fork.

5. Bake the crispbreads for about 10 minutes, turning the trays halfway through the cooking time. Allow them to cool on a wire rack before transferring to an airtight container.

These flatbreads are best enjoyed and eaten as soon as they have finished cooking. Clapping the cooked flatbread releases the steam trapped inside, creating a softer, flakier texture.

Whole Wheat Flatbreads

1. Sift the flour, baking powder, and salt into a bowl, shaking in any bran that may be left in the sieve. Add the butter and rub it in with your fingertips, until the mixture resembles fine breadcrumbs. Make a well in the center and stir in 6 tablespoons of water to make a firm but pliable dough.

2. Turn the dough out onto a lightly floured surface and knead it for a few minutes until it is smooth. Divide the dough into 4 balls, flatten them slightly, and then roll each one out into rounds, no more than $1/8$-inch thick. Brush each round with oil and fold it in half, then in half again. Roll the dough back into balls, and then roll it out into rounds again, as above.

3. Heat a large, heavy-bottom frying pan over medium heat. Working one at a time, brush each flatbread with a little oil on both sides, and then add it to the hot pan. Cook each flatbread for 3–4 minutes, turning it frequently, and brushing it with oil each time you do so.

4. Remove the flatbread from the pan, place it in the your palm of your hand and clap your hands together 3–4 times, taking care not to burn yourself. Wrap the flatbread in a clean dish towel and keep it warm while you cook the rest.

Makes 4

2 cups whole wheat flour, plus extra for dusting

1 tsp baking powder

1 tsp fine sea salt

3½ tbsps butter, diced and chilled

Vegetable oil, for brushing

Roasted Spiced Chickpeas

These are ridiculously addictive to snack on as is, but they are also great added to salads to give crunch and spice. You won't look at chickpeas in the same way from here on in!

Serves 4

2 14-oz cans chickpeas, drained and rinsed

2 tbsps olive oil

½ tsp cayenne pepper

½ tbsp smoked paprika

1 tsp ground cumin

1 tbsp sea salt

1. Preheat the oven to 400°F (350°F fan).

2. Toss all the ingredients in a bowl until completely coated, and then spread the spiced chickpeas out on a large roasting tray in a single layer. Roast them in the oven for 35–40 minutes, or until they're crisp.

3. These are best served still warm from the oven. Alternatively, cook them several hours in advance and then reheat them at the same temperature for 10 minutes.

Sweet Potato Fries

Hands down, these are one of my favorite snacks. They don't get as crispy as regular, homemade baked fries, but I love their sweet chewiness. To get them at all crispy, you do have to cook them just until they're slightly charred, so keep an eye on them right at the end. The sweet starchiness of these fries allows for bold spicing, so do experiment with spices like cayenne pepper, cumin, or chili powder.

Serves 2

3 medium sweet potatoes, cut lenghwise into ³/₈-inch-wide strips

1 tbsp vegetable oil

2 tsps Cajun seasoning or smoked paprika

3 thyme sprigs

Sea salt

1. Preheat the oven to 400°F (350°F fan).

2. Toss the sweet potato fries into a large roasting pan with the vegetable oil, Cajun seasoning, thyme, and sea salt, making sure they are well coated.

3. Pop the roasting pan into the oven for 35–40 minutes. Toss the fries halfway through the cooking time and keep an eye on them—you want them to be slightly charred at the edges. Serve immediately.

Root Vegetable Mash

I've taken to using coconut oil when I make a root vegetable mash like this one—not because of its rumored health benefits, but because, at its core, it has a sweet, exotic flavor that complements the vegetables and helps to create a smooth, velvety consistency when the root veggies are mashed. If you have time, slowly caramelize some sliced red onion in a pan over low heat, and then fold them through the mash—heaven!

Serves 4–6

2 lbs sweet potatoes, turnips, and
  parsnips, peeled and chopped into
  1-inch pieces
1–2 tbsps coconut oil
Sea salt and freshly ground black pepper

1. Place the vegetables in a large pot and fill it with enough cold water to cover them. Place the pot over high heat and bring it to a boil. Cook the vegetables for 15–20 minutes, or until the pieces are tender when pierced with a fork.

2. Drain the vegetables completely in a colander, then return them to the pot. Add the coconut oil, and mash the vegetables until they are completely smooth. Season them with salt and pepper and serve immediately.

Spiced yogurts feature a lot in my cooking lately—
I find them a great (and slightly healthier) alternative to
mayonnaise or sour cream. Use them to top salads, beans,
falafel, or as a dip for grilled meat or fish. Here are a few of
my favorite flavorings.

Spiced Yogurts

1. Whisk the yogurt and your chosen flavorings together in a bowl
until well combined.

2. Store in a covered bowl in the fridge until needed.

Serves 4

6 tbsps plain yogurt (preferably
   probiotic)

For sriracha yogurt
2 tsps sriracha sauce
1 garlic clove, very finely chopped

For Indian-spiced yogurt
1 tbsp hot curry powder
1 tsp ground turmeric

For herby yogurt
Large handful of mixed fresh herbs
   (cilantro, mint, basil), roughly
   chopped
1 garlic clove, very finely chopped

Roasted Cherry Tomatoes

I eat these roasted cherry tomatoes like sweets, warm from the oven. If I am ever left with a glut of tomatoes, I roast them just like this, and store them in a jar with olive oil. They are the perfect addition to salads or sandwiches, or to serve with grilled meats.

Serves 2–4

2 cups cherry tomatoes
2 tbsps olive oil
Sea salt and freshly ground black pepper

1. Preheat the oven to 400°F (350°F fan).

2. Slice the cherry tomatoes in half and place them, cut side up, in a roasting pan. Drizzle the tomatoes with the olive oil and season them with salt and pepper.

3. Roast the tomatoes in the oven for 30–35 minutes, or until they are reduced to half their size and have become slightly caramelized.

Grains 4 Ways

Quinoa

Serves 2

¾ cup plus 2 tbsps quinoa

1½ cups vegetable stock or water

1. Place the quinoa in a pan with the vegetable stock or water.

2. Bring to a boil over medium-high heat and cook for 15 minutes, or until the quinoa is tender, but still has some bite. Drain away any excess water before serving.

Bulgur Wheat

Serves 2

⅓ cup bulgur wheat

1. Place the bulgur wheat in a pan and cover it with cold water. Place the pan over medium-high heat and bring it to a boil.

2. Reduce the heat, cover the pan, and simmer for 8 minutes, or until the grains are tender. Drain before serving.

Grains are a big part of my diet, not only because of their nutritional content, but also because they bulk up many great dishes while also being fairly inexpensive. They are easy to cook and store ahead of time so they can be added to salads and served alongside meat and fish.

Green Lentils

Serves 2

⅔ cup dried green lentils

1. Rinse the lentils in cold water until the water runs clear, and then drain the lentils. Place them in a pan and cover them with cold water, to come about 2 inches above the level of the lentils.

2. Bring to a boil over medium-high heat, then reduce the heat and simmer for about 15–20 minutes, or until the lentils are tender but still have a little bite. Drain before serving.

Pearl Barley

Serves 2

¾ cup pearl barley

1. Place the pearl barley in a pan and cover it with water. Place the pan over medium-high heat and bring it to a boil.

2. Reduce the heat and simmer for 50 minutes, or until the grains are tender. Drain before serving.

Index

Note: Page numbers in *italics* indicate photos on pages separate from recipes.

STERLING EPICURE
New York

An Imprint of Sterling Publishing Co., Inc.
1166 Avenue of the Americas
New York, NY 10036

STERLING EPICURE and the distinctive Sterling logo are registered trademarks of Sterling Publishing Co., Inc.

This edition published in 2017 by Sterling Publishing Co., Inc.

First published in Great Britain in 2015 by Hodder & Stoughton, a Hachette UK company.

Text and photography © 2015 by Donal Skehan, except as noted at the bottom of this page
Illustrations © 2015 by Sarah Leuzzi

ISBN 978-1-4549-2304-6

Distributed in Canada by Sterling Publishing Co., Inc.
ᶜ/o Canadian Manda Group, 664 Annette Street
Toronto, Ontario, Canada M6S 2C8

For information about custom editions, special sales, and premium and corporate purchases, please contact Sterling Special Sales at 800-805-5489 or specialsales@sterlingpublishing.com.

Manufactured in Canada

10 9 8 7 6 5 4 3 2 1

www.sterlingpublishing.com

Additional photography: pages 9, 13, and 102 © 2015 by James Byrne; page 4 © 2015 by Rhianne Jones; pages 11, 16, 46, 72, 148, and 194 © 2015 by Sofie Larsson

Acknowledgments

Even after working on five cookbooks, I can tell you that the excitement of producing one still hasn't left me! I'm incredibly proud of this one, and it's particularly close to my heart. There is a huge amount of work that goes on behind the scenes, and for that I am so thankful to everyone who has helped make this book what it is. A huge and heartfelt thank you to:

My U.S. Dream Team at Sterling: The absolutely fabulous Marilyn Kretzer and Jennifer Williams. The ever-patient Blanca Oliviery and Elizabeth Lindy.

My U.S. agent: Jason Gutman and the team at Gersh.

Food Network Team: Jen Quaintain and Mark Levine.

My publicist: Amy Brownstein.

My U.K. editor: Sarah Hammond and all at Hodder & Stoughton.

My U.K. agent: Rosemary Scoular and the team at United Agents.

Recipe editor and tester: Orla Broderick and Sarah Watchorn.

TV team: Robin Murray and Marc Dillon at Appetite.

Food stylist and assistant, and prop stylist: Lizzie Kamenetzky, Poppy Mahon, and Polly Rawlings.

The HomeCooked Team: Sofie Larsson, Joanna Carley, and Max the dog.

Portrait photography: James Byrne.

And of course to my friends, family, and my wife Sofie, who make it all worthwhile.

A special thank you also to James, Craig, and baby Joshua, who put up with me writing while we stayed with them in L.A.

For more recipes visit:

donalskehan.com
youtube.com/donalskehan

And find me on Twitter, Facebook, Instagram, Pinterest, and SnapChat: DonalSkehan